To

OUR HONORED DEAD

*This book is reverently
dedicated*

Published by Books Express Publishing
Copyright © Books Express, 2011
ISBN 978-1-78039-122-9

Books Express publications are available from all good retail and online booksellers. For publishing proposals and direct ordering please contact us at: info@books-express.com

THE STORY OF A REGIMENT

IN ACTION

Newspaper Clippings Collage

MacArthur Returns to the Philippines with 225,000 Japanese Veteran Fighters

- Landings On Leyte
- Split Forces Of Enemy — Huge Convoy Pours Supplies Ashore As Beachheads Are Expanded
- YANKS MAKE NEW GAINS IN LEYTE DRIVE
- U.S. Vets Drive Over Mountain, Surprise Japs
- JAPAN LANDS 10,000 MORE FRESH TROOPS
- Opposing Armies On Leyte Bogged Down By Tropical Typhoon
- JAPS FIGHTING BITTERLY FOR ORMOC SECTOR
- MacArthur Sweeps 15 Towns; MacArthur Holds 40-Mile Leyte Coast
- *Yamashi!* Begins Battle
- Japs Belittle Philippine Attack
- YANK FORCES DRIVE NEARLY ACROSS LEYTE
- Nosara Must Be Drinking That Sake, Too
- CENTRAL PHILIPPINES, ISLANDS FIRMLY HELD
- Yanks Destroy 600 Nipponese In North Leyte
- New Trap Set To Annihilate Leyte Force
- Jap Unit in Ormoc Sector Surrounded By 24th Division
- NEW TRAP IS SET FOR FOE ON LEYTE
- Americans Advance On Leyte

Juichi Terauchi — Jap Adversary of MacArthur

TABLE OF CONTENTS

	Page
Foreword	1
The 21st Infantry Trophy of Niagara	2
Explanatory Note	3
Regimental Coat of Arms	4
21st Infantry Anthem	7
Battle Honors	8
Battle Honors, World War II	9
Map Southern Pacific Area	10
Pearl Harbor and the Early Days	17
Hollandia, New Guinea	18
Sixth U. S. Army - By Gen. Walter Krueger	24
X Corps - Leyte - By Maj. Gen. F. C. Sibert	26
Commendation by Commanding General 24th Division	28
The 21st R.C.T. on Leyte	29
The Chain of Command - Leyte	30
Roster of Officers, 21st Infantry, 20 Oct. 1944	34
Breakneck Ridge - Limon, Sketch Map	39
Breakneck Ridge Offensive	42
Map - Breakneck Ridge, Leyte	43
Clipping from Japanese Press in Manila	77
Enemy Tactics, Leyte	90
Commendation, 6 December 1944	95
Daro, Carigara and Mindoro	97
Mindoro Song	104
Guerrilla Reports - Mindoro	105
Distinguished Unit Citation, Cannon Company	109
Lubang	110
Roster of Officers, 10 March 1945	114
Their Last Stronghold - By Maj. Gen. R. B. Woodruff	122
Davao Campaign	125
Calender of Mindanao Campaign	127
Map, Parang - Cotobato Area	128
Map, Davao Area, Mindanao	133
General Orders No. 23, 1946 - James H. Diamond	143
News Accounts - Captain Theodore Crouch	148
News Accounts - 21st Infantry	149
Captain Theodore Crouch	152
Commendation, 20 June 1945	156
Japanese Order of Battle - Davao	157
Jock Clifford	159
General Orders No. 79, Hq. X Corps	160
Poem, August 14, 1945 - by W. J. Verbeck	161
Things to Remember	162
To the Regimental Medical Detachment	165
Decorations	166
The Field of Honor - Killed in Action and Died of Wounds, 21st Infantry	172

The narrative accounts of the work are, for the most part, taken from official records. The events narrated, although of some interest, lack color and descriptive effect. Human interest is practically lacking. In order to tell the story with a proper background it would be necessary to obtain personal experience narratives from hundreds of enlisted men and officers to cover the actual combat description of each small unit on each battlefield. In order to more vividly describe the true picture existing during the various actions, certain citations for awards and decorations are inserted. The citations inserted are in a smaller type and written on separate pages so as not to interrupt the continuity of the basic narrative. The citations inserted are but a small percentage of those awarded for each phase of a battle. Unfortunately they are the only ones available to the writer. They will, however, serve to describe the intensity of the combat and to insert human interest into the reading.

Between 1815 and 1861 there was no Twenty-first Infantry Regiment. Our predecessors during the War of 1812, however, established a foundation for the elan which we bear now and always. Here is an account of the gimlets of one hundred and thirty-two years ago.

THE 21st INFANTRY'S TROPHY OF NIAGARA

THE Battle of Niagara, fought within sight of Niagara Falls, is perhaps better known to the student of history as the battle of Lundy's Lane. This latter name arises from the fact that the bitterest part of the struggle occurred in Lundy's Lane during the attack by the American Infantry on the British battery which was in position there. The following account of the battle is taken from a history of the 21st Infantry, published by Capt. C. E. Hampton, 21st Infantry, in 1909:

At sunset, on the evening of July 25th, 1814, General Winfield Scott's brigade, advancing down the Niagara River, on the Canadian side, found itself confronted by the British Army drawn up on rising ground a short distance below the Falls. Although greatly outnumbered and overmatched in artillery, Scott unhesitatingly engaged the enemy and sent word to General Brown, at Chippewa, of the perilous situation. The latter ordered General Ripley forward and hastened to the battlefield. At nine o'clock, p. m., Ripley's brigade, consisting of the Twenty-first and Twenty-third Infantry regiments, with a detachment of the First, arrived upon the scene. Scott's troops were exhausted and scattered by the continuous fighting, and Ripley's were at once pushed forward to form a new line.

A British battery of seven guns posted on a hill in the center of their line, near a road called Lundy's Lane, was seen to be the key to their position. Turning to Colonel James Miller, who commanded the Twenty-first Infantry, General Brown said: "Colonel, take your regiment, storm that work, and take it." Colonel Miller's prompt reply, "I'll try, sir," is one of the few sentient speeches of the battlefield that our history has delighted to transmit from generation to generation.

In the dim moonlight the Twenty-first climbed the hill until it reached a rail fence near the battery. Resting their muskets on this fence, our men poured in a volley that killed or wounded every one of the gunners, then rushed the battery and took possession of their guns. A British line, lying in support, fired with deadly effect and then charged, with intent to retake the guns with the bayonet but were driven back. Three times they made desperate efforts to recapture the battery, but the Twenty-first doggedly held its ground. The combatants were so close that the fire from their muskets crossed and it is said that the buttons on the enemies' uniforms could be plainly distinguished by its light. The Twenty-first suffered fearful losses and must inevitably have been expelled from its hard won position had not Ripley, with the First and Twenty-htird, come to its aid. The enemy, having also been heavily re-enforced, made three more unsuccessful assaults, and then retired from the field.

General Brown complimented the regiment and its commander in the highest terms and presented to it one of the captured guns, a beautiful bronze six-pounder, "in testimony of its distinguished gallantry." In addressing Colonel Miller he said, "You have immortalized yourself"; and passing years have proved his prophecy correct.

In this desperate struggle the Twenty-first lost one hundred and twenty-six killed and wounded, or forty-five per cent. of its entire strength, the regiment having entered with less than three hundred men.

The battle was won against odds of almost two to one, and from a foe that numbered in his ranks many of Wellington's veterans, trained on the battlefields of the Spanish Peninsula. As example of calculating courage, of tenacious persistence, and of headlong bravery, our history contains none more brilliant, nor is it likely to show, in the future, one more glorious. Time cannot dim the luster of such deeds.

(From "The Story of a Regiment" by Judson MacIvor Smith)

EXPLANATORY NOTE

Until comparatively recent years no effort has been made systematically to continue in unbroken service the regular regiments of the army. Thus at the close of most of our wars regiments have been disbanded and their existence brought to an untimely end, and a unit which fought in the War of 1812 and the Civil War, for example, under the same regimental designation, need not necessarily be in any sense whatever the same organization.

Thus, the story of the present 21st Infantry properly begins with G.O. #33, WD, dated June 18, 1861, which provides for the creation of the 12th Regiment of U. S. Infantry. Through the accident of common practice during the war, wherein battalions frequently served as separate and distinct units, our lineage is properly traced through the actions of the 2d Battalion, 12th Infantry, until the promulgation of G.O. #50 WD, dated August 1, 1866 and G.O. #92 dated November 23, 1866, which changed the name of the 2d Battalion, 12th Infantry, to the 21st Regiment of Infantry.

The 3d Battalion, 14th Infantry, which had not been organized during the Civil War, was organized and recruited to strength in the fall of 1865 and transferred to the Pacific Coast for service in Arizona. Pursuant to the same orders which changed the 2d Battalion, 12th Infantry, to the 21st Infantry, this 3d Battalion, 14th Infantry, became the 32d Regiment, and, finally in 1869, pursuant to WD G.O. #16 and #17, the 32d was consolidated with the 21st, the consolidated regiment retaining the designation of the 21st U. S. Infantry.

G.O. #33 WD, dated June 28, 1921, transferred all personnel of the 21st Infantry to other regiments and transferred the regiment, by means of its colors and records, to the Hawaiian Department.

G.O. #35, HD, dated August 19, 1921, directed that: "Upon arrival in the Department the Colors and Records will be sent to Schofield Barracks, T. H., and there turned over to the Commanding General of that post. Effective upon receipt, the entire personnel of the 44th Infantry is transferred to the 21st Infantry. The 44th Infantry is placed on the inactive list, with the 21st Infantry as its active associate.

REGIMENTAL COAT OF ARMS

HEADQUARTERS, 21st INFANTRY
Office Of The Regimental Commander,
Schofield Barracks, Hawaii

General Orders)   February 15, 1924.
No. 1   )

Subject: REGIMENTAL INSIGNIA.

Extract

1. General Orders No. 7, these headquarters, dated April 9, 1923, is revoked and the following regulations contained in a letter from the Adjutant General of the Army will hereafter govern the wearing of the 21st Infantry Regiment Distinctive Insignia by members of the command:

      .   o   .   .   .

1. The Secretary of War approves the following Coat-of-Arms for the 21st Regiment of Infantry for wear as part of the uniform of the Regiment.

Arms: Party per fess azure and argent, in chief a sun in splendor or charged with a five-bastioned fort of the first, in base a cedar tree eradicated proper.

Crest: On a wreath of the colors four arrows sable, armed and feathered gules, tied with a rattlesnake skin proper.

Motto: Duty.

Description: This regiment was originally organized in 1861 as the 2nd Battalion, 12th Infantry, and as such was in the Army of the Potomac, taking part in numerous engagements, the baptism of fire being at Cedar Mountain, August 9, 1862, where it performed its mission with such success as to bring forth special mention from General Prince, the Brigade Commander. This incident is shown by the cedar tree. In 1866 it was enlarged and the name changed to 21st Infantry. It was in four Indian Campaigns, shown by the four arrows of the crest, the rattlesnake was the Indian emblem of War. At Santiago, the regiment was in the 5th Corps, the badge of which was a five-bastioned fort, and its Philippine service is shown by the Katipunan sun. The colors of the shield, blue and white, have been the Infantry colors during the existence of the Regiment.

                                        By order of COLONEL PERRY:

                                                   (Signed)   W. C. DeWare,
                                                                               Adjutant.

GIMLETS HAVE FOUGHT IN THE PHILIPPINES BEFORE

21st INFANTRY ANTHEM

In 1916-1917, while the Regiment was engaged on Mexican Border duty, with headquarters in San Diego, California, it acquired an admiring friend in Carrie Jacobs Bond, famous American composer. The Blue Flag, a musical selection for band, was copyrighted by her in 1917. She published this selection and dedicated it to the 21st Infantry. The End of a Perfect Day, the author's best known composition, constitutes a part of The Blue Flag, and was dedicated as the Regimental Anthem at a meeting of the entire Regiment on September 16, 1937. The words of the anthem are by Margaret B. Woodward, wife of Second Lieutenant Lamar F. Woodward, 21st Infantry.

> To the glory of men who have gone before,
>   And the glory of sons yet unborn;
> The Twenty-first ever we consecrate,
>   May her crest long with honor be worn;
> United we'll stand whene'er duty calls,
>   To a man, till the vict'ry is won,
> And the fame and the strength of the Twenty-first
>   Shall be pride in the task well done.

BATTLE HONORS
21st Infantry

CIVIL WAR

Peninsula	Gettysburg
Virginia 1862	Virginia 1863
Manassas	Wilderness
Antietam	Spottsylvania
Fredericksburg	Cold Harbor
Chancellorsville	Petersburg

INDIAN WARS

Arizona 1866	Arizona 1870
Arizona 1867	Modoc
Arizona 1868	Nez Perces
Arizona 1869	Bannocks

SPANISH AMERICAN WAR

Santiago

PHILIPPINES INSURRECTION

Zapote River	Luzon 1901
Luzon 1899	Luzon 1902

WORLD WAR II.

Pearl Harbor, 7 December 1941
Tanahmerah Bay, New Guinea, 22 April 1944
Hollandia, New Guinea, 23-28 April 1944

Philippine Islands

Panaon Island, 20 October 1944
Breakneck Ridge, Leyte, 5-18 November 1944
Hill 1525, 8-9 November 1944 (1st Bn.)
Daro - Mt. Lao - Mt. Mamban, 20 November - 10 December 1944
Carigara Defensive, 10-27 December 1944
San Jose, Mindoro, 22-29 December 1944 (3rd Bn.)
San Jose, 29 December - 7 January 1945 (Remainder of Rgt.)
Boak, Maranduque, January 1945 (K Co.)
Pinamalayan, Mindoro, 7-11 January 1945 (I Co.)
Bongabong, 6-14 January 1945 (3rd Bn.)
Gusay, 20 January 1945
Calipan - Najuan, 20-24 January 1945
Nasugbu - Wawa - Lian - Tagaytay - Imus - Paranaque - Zapote -
Las Pinas - Nichols Field - Ft. Wm. McKinley - Alabang - Los Banos -
31 January - 3 March 1945 (Cannon Company)
Lubang Island, 28 February - 7 March 1945 (1st Bn.)
Dipolog, Mindanao, March 1945 (2nd Bn.)
Malabang - Parang, Mindanao, 17 April 1945
Cotobato, 18 April 1945 (2nd Bn.)
Tamontako - Lamopog, 18-19 April 1945 (2nd Bn.)
Toril - Bago, 2 May 1945
Mintal, 2-9 May 1945
Libby Drome, 3-13 May 1945
Talomo Heights, 10-13 May 1945 (1st Bn.)
Tugbok, 9-19 May 1945 (2nd Bn.)
Mintal - Ula Roads, 9-25 May 1945
Bayabas, 30-31 May 1945 (1st Bn.)
Mulig, 2 June 1945
Alhambre, 3 June 1945
Shankee, 3 June 1945
Monterey - Naming - Tagakpan - Talomo Valley, 3-13 June 1945
Wangan, 15 June 1945
Calinan, 18 June 1945
Baguio, 17-18 June 1945
Tamogan Trail, 6-19 June 1945
Tamogan Trail, 10 July - 1 August 1945
Sarangani Bay, 16 July - 7 August 1945 (1st Bn.)

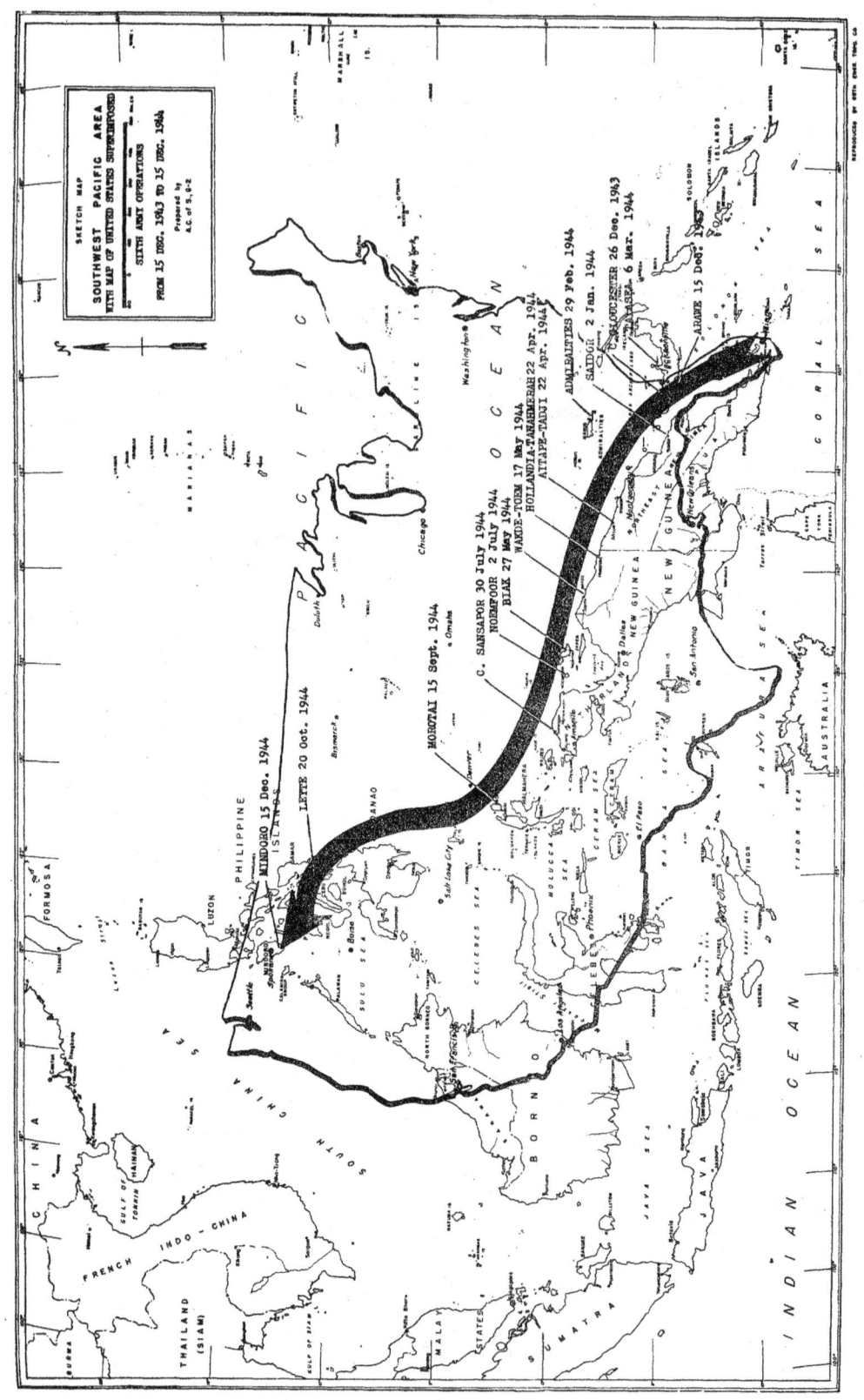

The Boss gave us his approval.

We were inspected at Rockhampton, Australia by Lieutenant General Walter Krueger and General Eichelberger. General Irving stands between Generals K and E. The Sergeant is Walter E. Scherer.

Colonel A. S. Newman, Chief of Staff, 24th Division, Major General Fred Irving, Commanding General of the division and Lt. Col. Fred R. Weber, 21st Infantry at Goodenough Island. Colonel Newman was seriously wounded while in command of the 34th Infantry Regiment at JARO, Leyte.

Lt. Col. F. R. Weber, executive officer of the 21st Infantry Regiment, Goodenough Island. Feb. 20, 1944.

Private Vengel S. Sotir, Company "B" cleans his rifle on the deck of the "ALLEN" en-route to the landing at HOLLANDIA, New Guinea.

Private First Class John Eadie, Anti-Tank Company, 21st Infantry crossing a stream during the invasion at Hollandia, New Guinea on April 22, 1944. We had a man drowned in this stream.

PEARL HARBOR AND THE EARLY DAYS

When the Japanese struck Pearl Harbor, the 24th Division was one of the two divisions garrisoned in the Hawiian Islands. This was December 7, 1941. The division suffered light casualties only. The division was composed basically of three regimental combat teams built around its three infantry regiments. Threse regiments were the 19th Infantry (Rock of Chikamauga), the 21st Infantry (Gimlets) and the 34th Infantry. The 24th Division was a Regular Army Division. The division immediately began to strengthen the defenses of Oahu and train for jungle warfare and amphibious landings.

When the threat to the islands had passed, the division sailed for the South Pacific, arriving at Rockhampton, Australia in August 1943. Then began another long period of training which was soon to bear its first fruit.

HOLLANDIA, NEW GUINEA

On 22 April 1944, D-Day for the Tanahmerah Bay-Hollandia Campaign, the Regiment launched its first campaign against the Japs. This invasion climaxed a long period of training and defensive action in Oahu, Australia, and Goodenough Island. The Gimlets smashed thru thirty-five miles of rough jungle terrain in four and a half days and fought one battle enroute. This campaign has since been rated as the fastest and best coordinated campaign in jungle warfare.

After a practice landing on the coast of New Guinea, the Gimlets loaded on transports and became part of a 850 ship convoy. Seven days later, on the morning of 22 April 1944, the Regiment landed at Tanahmerah and Depapre, New Guinea.

ACTION OF THE 21ST INFANTRY, 22 APRIL 1944

The 21st Infantry, commanded by Col. Charles Lyman, less the 1st Battalion, to land at Tanahmerah Bay, secure a beachhead, and move overland to Depapre. The 3rd Engineers to construct a road from Tanahmerah to Depapre. The 52nd Field Artillery to go into position at Tanahmerah Bay and be prepared to fire in support of the Regiment.

ACTION OF THE 1st BATTALION, 21ST INFANTRY

The 1st Battalion, 21st Infantry, was ordered to land at Depapre Bay, secure a beachhead, leave Company "A" to hold the beachhead until relieved by the 2nd Battalion, 21st Infantry. The 1st Battalion, less Company "A" to move out immediately and seize the Regimental objective, the high ground overlooking Depapre.

At 0830 the morning of 22 April 1944 the 1st Battalion, commanded by Lieut. Colonel Thomas (Jock) Clifford, had successfully established a beachhead at Depapre Bay. Company "A" quickly organized the defense of the beachhead and the remainder of the Battalion moved out toward Mariobe, the Regimental objective.

At 1600, 22 April, the 1st Battalion had seized Mariobe, and dug in for the night. The first day of the campaign had been uneventful with exception of a few Japs killed by naval fire, and two prisoners captured by a patrol from Company "C" lead by Lieut. Charles Counts. These were the first Jap prisoners to be captured by the Gimlets.

The landing of the Regiment at Tanahmerah was not so successful. The terrain that looked so good in aerial photos turned out to be impassable swamp. This beachhead had to be abandoned and the Regimental combat team moved by landing craft to the Depapre beachhead. A small detachment of the 2nd Battalion was sent overland from Tanahmerah to Depapre to reconnoiter the shore. The Depapre beachhead, although inadequate, became the beachhead of the entire 24th Division.

On the morning of 23 April the Gimlets bagged their first Jap. Pvt. Martin of Company "C", looking up from a breakfast of "K" ration, saw a Jap peering thru the bushes. A well aimed shot earned Martin the honor of being the first Gimlet to kill a Jap. This was number one on a list of many thousand doomed to stop Gimlet lead.

Eager to contact the enemy, the 1st Battalion pushed on. All morning of the 23rd of April Jap reconnaissance patrols moved parallel to our column but no contact was made. At 1500, 23 April 1944, the 2nd Platoon, Company "C", commanded by Lieut. Jack Wright, contacted and drove in a Jap outpost on Distassi Creek. Distassi Creek was named in honor of Sgt. Distassi, the first Gimlet killed in action against the Japs. The 2nd Platoon of Company "C" had engaged a strong enemy force estimated as two rifle companies reinforced.

The 1st Platoon, Company "C", commanded by Lieut. Robert (Ace) Malone, was ordered to envelop the enemy's left flank. Moving quickly the 1st Platoon overran a Jap outpost of twenty men, crossed the creek and drove to center of the enemy strong point where they met stubborn resistance. The weapons platoon of Company "C", commanded by Lieut. William Langford, went into action, made a direct hit on a Jap armored car and neutralized three machine gun nests. Company "C" was commanded by Captain Roy Marcy. Lieut. Phillip Irons lead a platoon of Company "B" up and moved into position on the right flank of Company "C". The small area was a hell of sound, gun flashes, and the hoarse shouts of men in battle.

At 1630 Colonel Clifford ordered the 1st Battalion into perimeter for the night. Just before dusk the Battalion was greeted by Father Brady, the Regimental Chaplain. He was making the rounds giving away cigarettes and words of encouragement. Chaplain Brady had gone ashore with the bulk of the regiment, but upon hearing that the 1st Battalion was in a fight, had made the hazardous trip up over the mountain to join the 1st Battalion.

That night the enemy pulled out of their defense on the creek, broke into small groups, and continued to harass our perimeter until dawn of the 24th.

The morning of 24 April patrols were sent out and reported that the enemy had withdrawn. At 0900 Company "A", having been relieved from the beachhead, rejoined the 1st Battalion and was sent across the creek to occupy the Jap position. Orders were received to hold our position until the Regiment could be consolidated and rations and ammunition brought forward. At 1100 the 3rd Battalion, 21st Infantry, joined the 1st Battalion.

At 0730, April 25th, the 1st Battalion continued the advance on Hollandia. The terrain opened up as we followed an improved road toward the drome. Enemy equipment and supplies had been abandoned beside the road as the terrified enemy hastily withdrew. In some houses tables were found set for meals that were never eaten. Occasionally a sniper would harass our column but never again did the enemy attempt to block our advance to Hollandia.

Gimlets cross another river in New Guinea.

Men of Company "L", 3rd Battalion, 21st Regimental Combat Team. They are just back from a Combat Patrol around Lake SENTANI. This was during the Hollandia Campaign in Dutch New Guinea.

SILVER STAR

Private Leo J. Burkard, 37 144140, Co. G., 21st Infantry, 24th Division. For gallantry in action approximately 800 yards northwest of EBELI PLANTATION, Dutch New Guinea, 5 May 1944. The patrol of which Private Burkard was a member contacted a Japanese force of approximately 20 men with rifles and automatic weapons. Although wounded during the fire fight that followed, Private Burkard continued to bring rifle fire upon the enemy until hit a second time when he was dislodged from his firing position and rolled over the side of the bank of a ravine toward the enemy. When being removed from the ravine he pleaded to be left behind rather than endanger the lives of his comrades. The complete disregard of his personal safety in an effort to complete the mission of his patrol reflects great credit upon Private Burkard and the Military Service.

A Patrol from Love Company of the Gimlet Regiment. This group made a trip to the Village of JENSIP with natives who were guides. This area had not been penetrated since the Dutch were driven out two years previously. Picture was made at MARAREND VILLAGE, Dutch New Guinea during the Hollandia Campaign on June 9, 1944.

At 1155, 26 April 1944, Company "C", the Advance Guard of the Regiment, pulled upon a high hill overlooking the Hollandia Drome. As far as the eye could see lay blasted planes. The Regimental Commander ordered the 3rd Battalion to pass thru the 1st Battalion and seize the Drome. The 3rd Battalion, commanded by Lieut.Colonel Chester A. Dahlen, moved across the Hollandia Drome and secured the field. Later in the day the 3rd Battalion sent a patrol on to the Cyclops Drome where contact was made between the 24th and 41st Divisions thus ending the campaign.

So far, I have described only the action of the lead battalion of the Regiment. To the 2nd Battalion, commanded by Lieut.Colonel Seymour E. Madison, fell the task of supplying the lead battalions. The track over the mountain proved impassable for vehicles, even for the G.I.'s friend, the jeep. Instead, Gimlets wanting to fight, found themselves lugging boxes of K rations and ammunition in a long file up the rugged trail to supply the battalions forming the spearhead. It was ignominious work for highly trained combat men, but to their credit.

The campaign was officially over but much fighting remained to be done. The Hollandia Invasion had isolated 60,000 Japs to the south. They of course would attempt to join the forces north of Hollandia. The avenue of escape to the north was canalized through the Hollandia area. Trail blocks were established on all trails and trail functions leading north. It was in this kind of action that Pvt. Monroe McGee of Company "C" distinguished himself. McGee contributed a total of 45 Japs, killed, to the Regimental list. He was often referred to as, "One Man Patrol McGee".

When the mop-up was completed, the enemy had lost 1771 killed, and a then unprecedented number of prisoners - 502. This number was shared equally by all battalions of the Regiment. The Regiment had suffered only 32 casualties during the entire campaign. The main part of the division remained at Hollandia until the time was ripe for the invasion of the Philippines.

SIXTH U. S. ARMY -- PACIFIC VETERAN

By General Walter Krueger, USA
Commanding General, Sixth Army

By mid-October 1944, Sixth Army had cleared Western New Britain of enemy forces, had reconquered the Admiralties, had completed its operations on the north coast of New Guinea, had seized and secured southeastern Morotai in the Halmaheras, and was enroute to Leyte Island to begin the liberation of the Philippines. In order to appreciate the operations which followed, it is necessary to understand General MacArthur's over-all plan for the Philippine Campaign. First, the Leyte Operation was to be undertaken to obtain naval, air and supply bases from which to provide support for future Philippine Campaigns; next, the plan called for a hop from Leyte across the Visayas to seize southwestern Mindoro so as to establish airfields within 125 miles of Manila Bay; and third, a landing was to be made in the Lingayen Gulf area of Luzon, followed by a rapid drive southward to seize the Central Plain-Manila area, to open Manila Bay to our shipping, and subsequently, to destroy hostile forces remaining on Luzon. All of these operations were assigned to Sixth Army and plans for their accomplishment were well under way by the time Sixth Army was enroute to Leyte.

The Leyte Operation was divided into three tactical phases. Phase One consisted of an amphibious operation to secure the entrances to Leyte Gulf. Phase Two comprised major amphibious assaults: to seize the coastal strip of eastern Leyte from Tacloban to Dulag, including the airdromes and base sites in the area; to open San Juanico Strait and Panaon Strait; and to secure the central valley of Leyte including the Carigara Bay area on the north central coast. Phase Three called for the destruction of hostile forces remaining on Leyte and the clearing of hostile forces from southern Samar. Phase One of this operation lasted from 17-19 October 1944, during which time the 6th Ranger Infantry Battalion occupied Dinagat, Homonhon and Suluan Islands, thus securing the entrance to Leyte Gulf. Phase Two was initiated on 20 October 1944 when X Corps and XXIV Corps landed on the east coast of Leyte in a powerful amphibious assault. These landings followed by one hour the landing of the 21st Infantry Regiment of the 24th Infantry Division on Panaon Island, where this regiment rapidly established control over Panaon Strait.

Sixth Army quickly exploited its initial successes. In the X Corps zone of action the 1st Cavalry Division on 20 October seized Tacloban Airfield and on the following day captured Tacloban. Five days later elements of this division were moving northwestward along San Juanico Strait toward Carigara. The 24th Infantry Division secured Palo on 21 October, then advanced rapidly into the Leyte Valley, and on 29 October succeeded in gaining contact with elements of the 1st Cavalry Division south of Carigara. In a coordinated attack by units of these two divisions Carigara was captured 2 November.

Meanwhile, in the XXIV Corps zone of action, the 7th Infantry Division captured Dulag airstrip on 21 October, advanced rapidly westward to seize the three airfields in the Burauen area by 25 October, and captured Dagami on 29 October against heavy enemy resistance. Other elements of this division pushed southward, secured Abuyog and then advanced westward across the mountains to occupy Baybay on the Camotes Sea. The 96th Infantry Division, which had landed on the right of the 7th Infantry Division, initially by-passed enemy positions on Catmon Hill and seized the southern portion of the Leyte Valley within its zone of action. This division attacked Catmon Hill on 28 October and by 31 October had completely eliminated all enemy resistance there. Following this action, the 96th Infantry Division began the relief of the 7th Infantry Division in the Dulag-Burauen-Dagami-Tanauan area.

By 2 November 1944, Sixth Army had gained control of the broad Leyte Valley and its airfields, had opened Panaon and San Juanico Straits, and had secured Carigara on the north central coast and Baybay on the west coast, thus successfully completing the second phase of the operation. It soon developed, however, that General Yamashita, the Japanese commander in the Philippines, intended to hold Leyte at all costs. The Japanese High Command had already committed its navy in a bold and desperate attempt to defeat our naval forces in Philippine waters and destroy our shipping in Leyte Gulf. In the historic Battle of Leyte Gulf which occurred during the period 24-26 October, this threat was turned back by our Third and Seventh Fleets. A large part of the enemy naval forces were sunk and the remainder withdrew in a badly damaged condition.

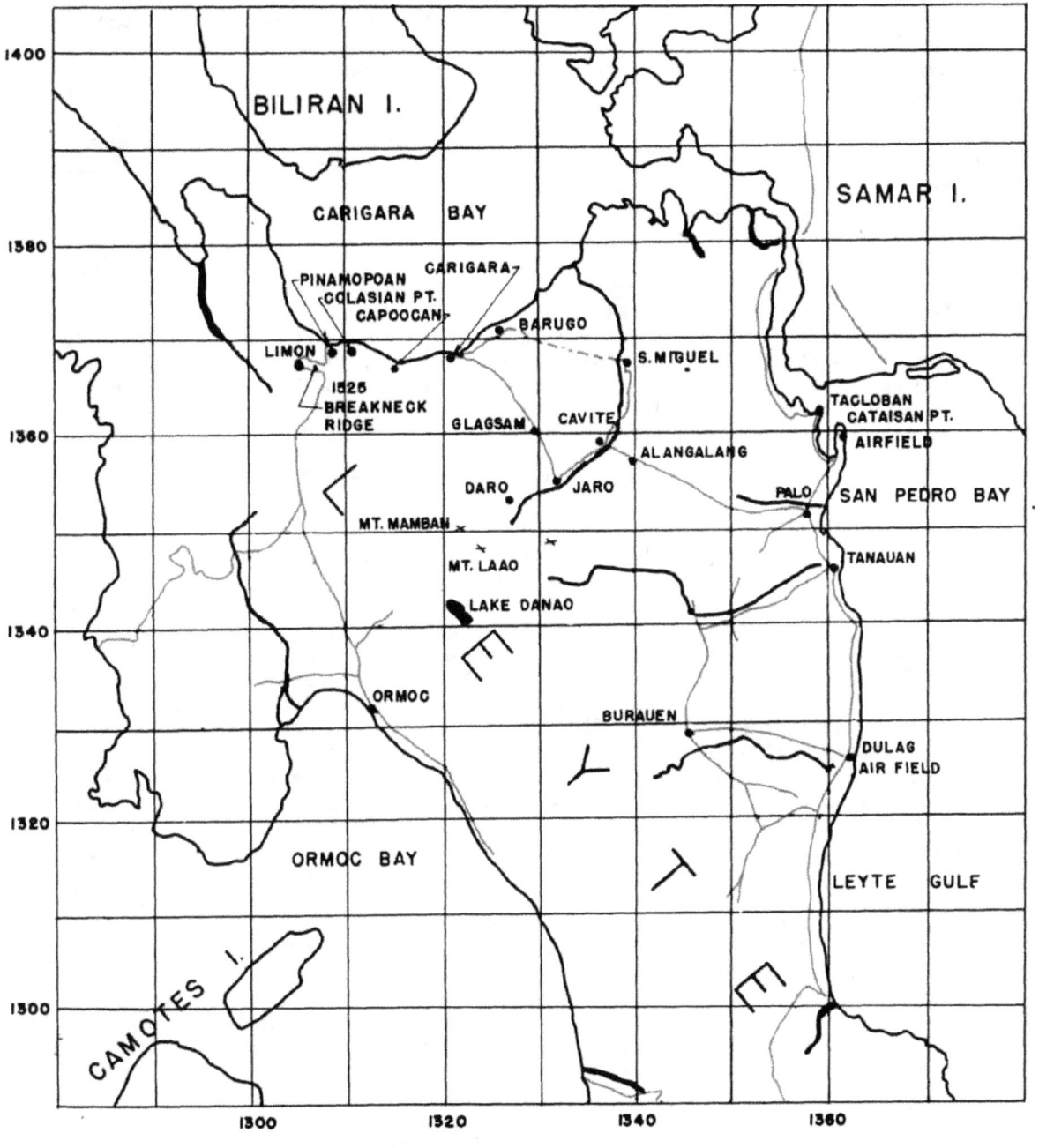

In spite of this disastrous naval defeat, General Yamashita rushed reinforcements to Leyte on all available craft, openly stating that the battle of the Philippines would be won or lost on Leyte Island. From Cebu, Panay, and Mindanao, enemy reinforcements came in barges, landing craft and other minor shipping; and from Luzon reinforcements poured southward in cruisers, destroyers, destroyer escorts and transports. In spite of terrific losses inflicted by our air attacks on his convoys, the enemy succeeded in landing a corps headquarters, and the bulk of five divisions, besides a considerable number of corps, combat and service troops. By early November, it was clearly apparent that Phase Three of the operation would be difficult and protracted, due not only to the heavy reinforcements which the enemy was rushing to Leyte, but also to the advent of the rainy season and to a lack of adequate air support caused by our inability to build airfields in the morass that Leyte had become.

Phase Three began on 3 November when X Corps advanced the 24th Infantry Division westward from its positions at Carigara. This division captured Pinamopoan on 4 November and then turned southward on Highway 2 in the direction of Ormoc. Shortly thereafter, it encountered strong and stubborn resistance on Breakneck Ridge which was not eliminated until 16 November.

End of Excerpt from General Kruger's Report.

X CORPS -- LEYTE
By Major General F. C. Sibert, USA
Commanding General, X Corps

X Corps, under Sixth Army, in its first operation landed on Leyte on 20 October 1944 in the first and decisive battle of the Philippines.

Its initial objectives, the seizure of Tacloban, Tacloban Airstrip, Palo, juncture with the XXIV Corps, and the opening of the San Juanico Strait, were accomplished in five bloody days in the midst of thousands of friendly filipinos and one typhoon.

By the twelfth day, the final Corps objective was taken when the 24th Infantry Division, driving up Leyte Valley, coordinated with the 1st Cavalry Division in a combined attack on Carigara. Elements of the 16th Japanese Division had been badly mauled and remnants driven into the hills between Ormoc Valley and Leyte Valley. The first of the Japanese reinforcements were met in the center of the valley at Jaro where elements of the Japanese 30th Division from Mindanao and elements of the 102d Japanese Division from Cebu were kicked aside by the 24th Infantry Division.

Japanese reinforcements were now pouring into Ormoc and the Corps was given the mission of advancing to secure that Port. The 24th Infantry Division advanced west along Carigara Bay and turned south on the highway towards Limon and Ormoc. The 1st Cavalry Division moved into the hills between the two valleys to prevent any hostile attempt to cross into Leyte Valley.

On turning south towards Limon, the 24th Infantry Division had a meeting engagement with the crack Japanese 1st Division and a gruelling fight ensued before the 24th Infantry Division finally overran the Japanese main position (Breakneck Ridge).

End of Excerpt from General Sibert's Report.

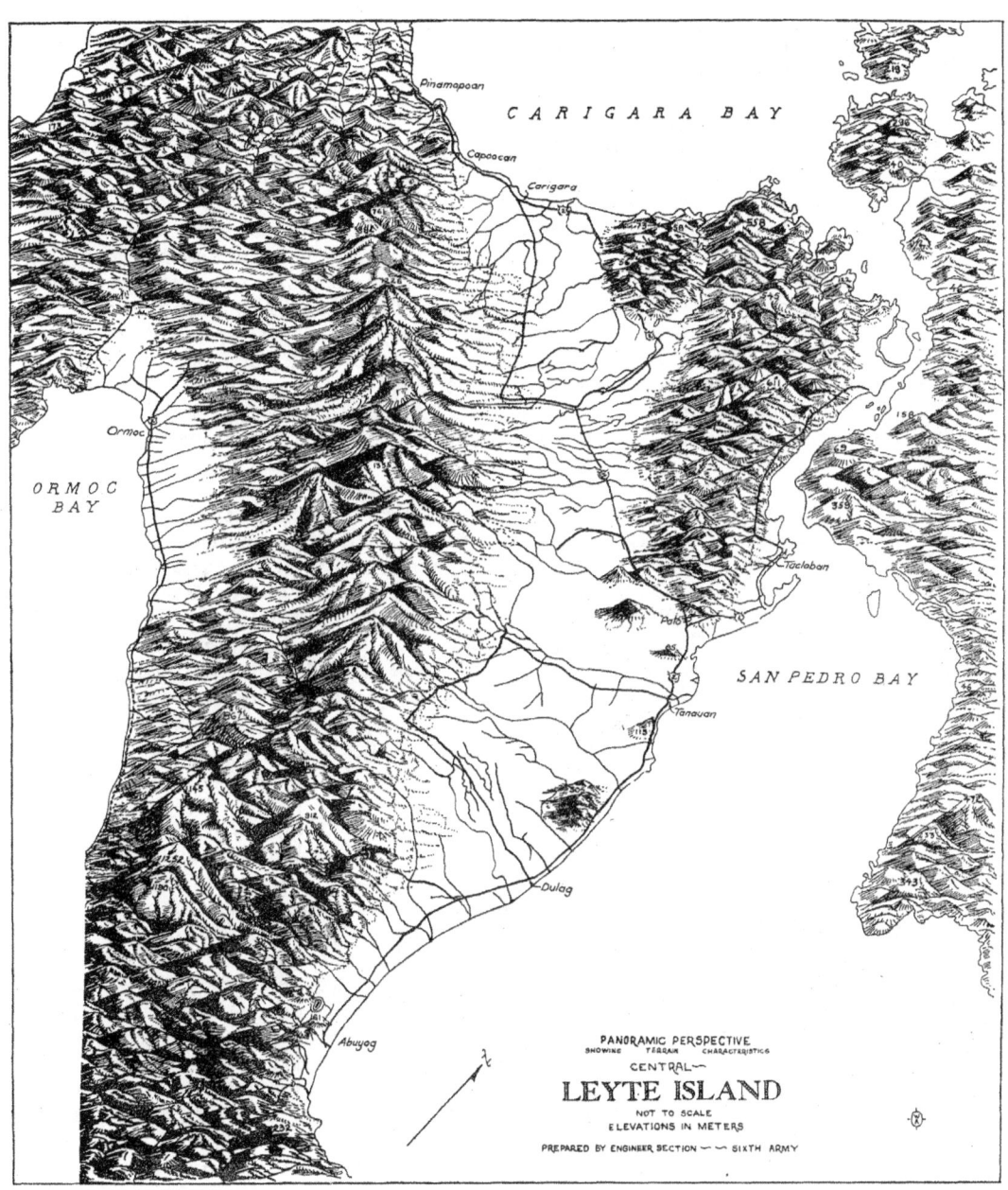

COMMENDATION BY THE COMMANDING GENERAL
24th DIVISION

The 21st Infantry Regiment is cited for extraordinary heroism and outstanding performance of duty in action against the enemy for 6 to 16 November 1944, and from 1 May to 19 June 1945, on Leyte and Mindanao Islands.

On 6 November 1944, the Regiment launched the first of a relentless series of attacks against Breakneck Ridge, key to the enemy defense system at the head of the Ormoc Corridor. Despite almost constant rain; the enemy's through exploitation of nearly perfect defensive terrain; meagre and uncertain supply, and dwindling reserves of manpower as compared with the enemy's constant reinforcement, the 21st Infantry took the offensive and held it against a veteran enemy force. By frontal attack and envelopment, the 21st maintained such pressure against a numerically superior enemy, that in twelve days it advanced 2000 yards and seized complete control of the dominating high ground. The Regiment counted a total of 1,779 enemy dead, an irreparable blow to one of the Japanese Empire's finest divisions. Undoubtedly many others lay undiscovered in the tangled terrain. This bitter and sustained struggle broke the enemy hold on the northern end of the Ormoc Valley and paved the way for the subsequent capture of Limon and the ultimate neutralization of the entire island. So severe had been the fighting that every third line soldier was either killed or wounded. Seven rifle company commanders fell. The Regiment then aided, after a short rest, in the annihilation of the enemy on Mindoro, Marinduque, Lubang, and Luzon. It struck Mindanao on 17 April as an assault unit of the 24th Division, seized the Malabang Airstrip and the key river port of Cotabato, and took part in the Division's lightning drive across the island. On 1 May, commencing at Bago, 140 miles from its starting point, the Regiment attacked 6,500 Japanese troops concentrated in the Talomo River Valley. These elements were strongly supported by artillery, armed with an inordinately high proportion of automatic weapons, and manning expertly placed positions, built over a period of years, and naturally camouflaged by lush tropical growth. For fifty-one heat-ridden days, with thick abaca fields channelizing its attacks, but permitting strong infiltration against its flanks and rear, the 21st continued the indomitable assault. After fourteen days it was able to commit only 54% of its original strength, but it never relaxed pressure. Without losing momentum, it absorbed 1000 replacements. By 18 June the Regiment had advanced twelve miles, taken the finest airfield on Davao Gulf, killed by actual count 2,133 enemy troops, disorganized and scattered the remainder and destroyed or captured all of their organic equipment. In addition to its heavy battle casualties, the attrition of severe heat, difficult terrain and continued strain had forced hospitalization of 1,411 other officers and men. During the gruelling period every assigned objective was taken on schedule. The fierce fighting spirit of the Regiment communicated itself to every man, old and new alike, and morale remained grimly high. These actions of the 21st Infantry Regiment reflect the finest traditions of the United States Army and will stand as a bright page in the nation's military history.

ROSCOE B. WOODRUFF
Major General
Commanding.

THE TWENTY FIRST REGIMENTAL COMBAT TEAM
(On Leyte)

21st Infantry Regiment
52nd Field Artillery Battalion
1st Platoon, Company A, 3rd Engineers
Collecting Company A, 24th Medical Rgt.
Company A, 44th Tank Battalion
Company C, 632nd Tank Destroyer Battalion
Company C, 85th Chemical Battalion (4.2" mortars)
7th Portable Surgical Hospital

After the battle of Breakneck Ridge the RCT was changed from time to time to include other Engineer Units, new Portable Surgical Hospitals, and tank and TD units, but the 52nd Field Artillery - a magnificient battalion of 105mm howitzers - remained with the 21st Infantry throughout all the fighting in the Philippines except for a few weeks at Caragara when the 63rd Field Artillery Battalion was substituted.

It is desired here to pay tribute to the 52nd Field Artillery Battalion. No one knows more than the infantryman in battle how much we rely on our own artillery. The 52nd was always there with its guns to support us with its accurate and heavy fire for every step of our advance. Their forward observers were always with the most advanced infantrymen and performed acts of gallantry daily. Their guns were always our closest friends. Many a dead Jap claimed on the scoresheet of the 21st Infantry was really killed by our brothers of the 52nd. Many a soldier owes his life to them. Every honor which we claim for the 21st Infantry Regiment we gladly share with the 52nd Field Artillery Battalion.

The CHAIN OF COMMAND
for the
LEYTE ISLAND OPERATION
General DOUGLAS MacARTHUR

Commanding General Southwest Pacific Theater
Lieutenant General WALTER KRUEGER

Commanding General Sixth Army
Major General FRANKLIN C. SIBERT

Commanding General X Corps
Major General FREDERICK A. IRVING (prior to 17 Nov 44)
Major General ROSCOE B. WOODRUFF (after 17 Nov 44)

Commanding Generals 24th Division Landing Team
Brigadier General WILLIAM B. GRUBER

Commanding General 24th Division Artillery

Infantry Regimental Commanders

19th Infantry
Lt. Col. GEORGE R. CHAPMAN, Jr.

1st Battalion
Lt. Col. FREDERICK H. ZIERATH

2nd Battalion
Lt. Col. ROBERT B. SPRAGINS

3rd Battalion
Major ELMER C. HOWARD

13th F.A. Battalion
Lt. Col. HAROLD E. LIEBE

3rd Engineer Battalion
Major JOHN G. STARR (prior to 12 Nov 44)
Lt. Col. JOHN S. B. DICK (after 12 Nov 44)

24th Quartermaster Company
1st Lt. GEORGE SUMMERS (prior to 26 Oct 44)
1st Lt. LEONARD LEVITT (26 Oct to 14 Dec 44)
1st Lt. JOHN P. ROWLAND (after 14 Dec 44)

727th Amphibious Tractor Battalion
Major FRANK R. McLAVY

603rd Medium Tank Company
Capt. RICHARD B. THIEROLF

34th Infantry
Colonel AUBREY S. NEWMAN (prior to 31 Oct 44)
Lt. Col. CHESTER A. DAHLEN (31 Oct to 24 Dec 44)
Colonel WILLIAM W. JENNA (after 24 Dec 44)

1st Battalion
Major EDWIN M. EDRIS (prior to 23 Oct 44)
Major HENRY G. GOGIO, Jr. (23 Oct to 26 Oct 44)
Lt. Col. THOMAS E. CLIFFORD, Jr. (after 26 Oct 44)

2nd Battalion
Lt. Col. JAMES F. PEARSALL, Jr.

3rd Battalion
Lt. Col. EDWARD M. POSTLETHWAIT

532nd Engineer Boat and Shore Regimental Commander
Colonel ALEXANDER M. NEILSON

Artillery Battalion Commanders

63rd F.A. Battalion
Lt. Col. CORNELIS G.W. LANG

11th F.A. Battalion
Lt. Col. JOSEPH H. HODGES, Jr.

24th Cavalry Reconnaissance Troop
1st Lt. RICHARD V. COLLOPY

24th Signal Company
1st Lt. HARLEY E. CLAYTON

632nd Tank Destroyer Battalion
Lt. Col. HUGH M. FANNING

44th Medium Tank Battalion
Lt. Col. TOM H. ROSS

21st Infantry
Lt. Col. FREDERICK R. WEBER (prior to 7 Nov 44)
Colonel WILLIAM J. VERBECK (after 7 Nov 44)

1st Battalion
Major JOHN P. LEAHY (prior to 8 Nov 44)
Major LAMAR W. LITTLE (after 8 Nov 44)

2nd Battalion
Lt. Col. SEYMOUR MADISON

3rd Battalion
Lt. Col. ERIC F. RANKE

52nd F.A. Battalion
Major KENDEL K. HLACKER

24th Medical Battalion
Major JOHN M. PALMER

724th Ordnance Company
Capt. LESTER J. RINGENBERG (prior to 6 Nov 44)
Capt. HOWARD RICHARDSON (after 6 Nov 44)

85th Chemical Battalion
Major JOHN L. CARSON

158th Ordnance Bomb Disposal Squadron
1st Lt. FRANK C. TITLOW

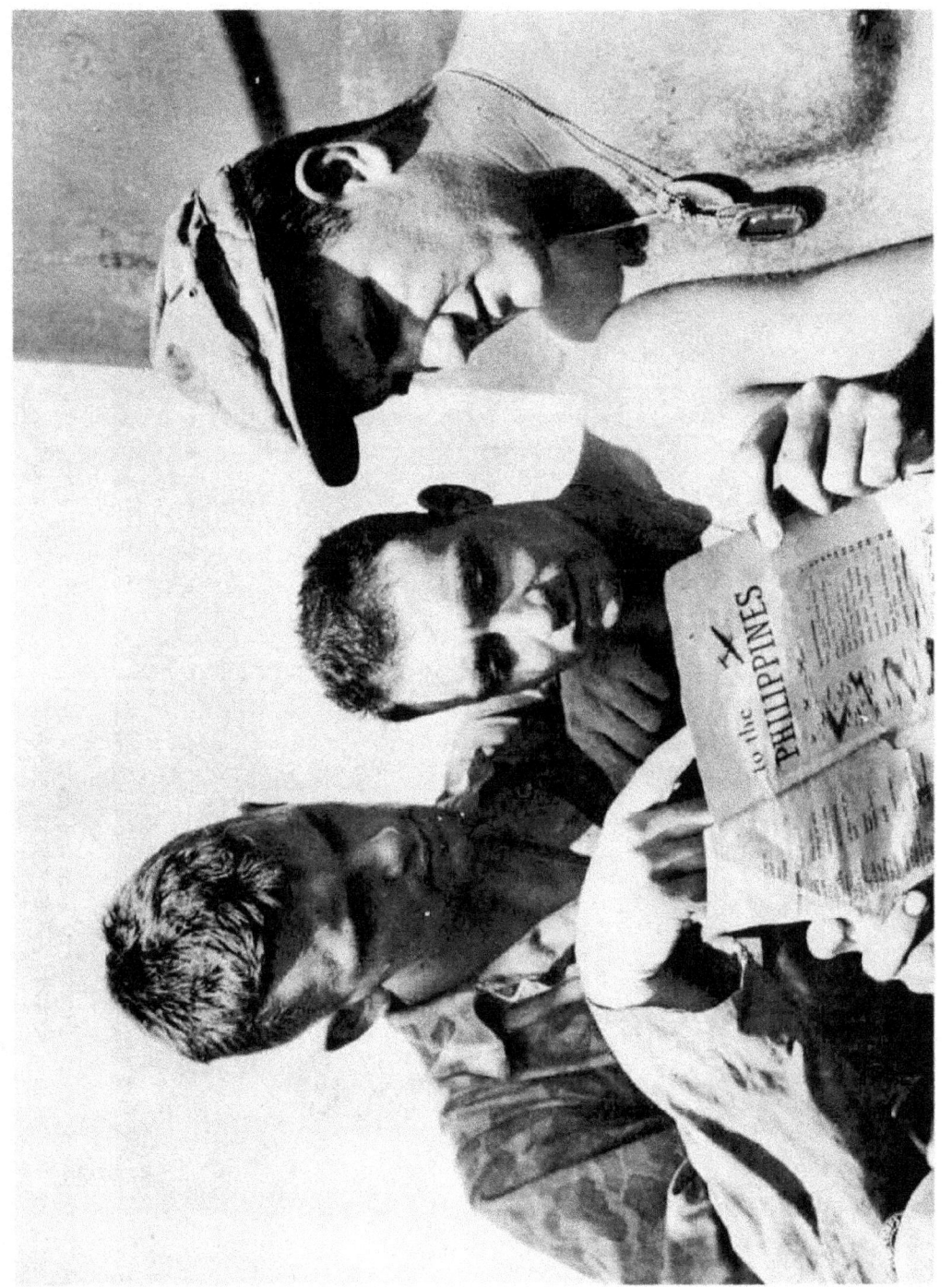

Gimlets en-route to the Philippines. October 18, 1944.

BAKER Company, 21st Infantry, Landing on D - Day, October 20, 1944, The Philippines. The 21st Infantry landed on PANAON, SOUTH LEYTE, DINAGAT and HOMONHON Islands.

Charley Company on "D" Day. Landing Southern Leyte on October 20, 1944.

ROSTER OF OFFICERS ASSIGNED
TO 21ST INFANTRY AS OF 20 OCTOBER 1944

Able, Sothoron K.	1st Lt.	Co. I. Plat. Ldr.
Aitken, Malcom D.	Capt.	Hq. 3d Bn., Bn. S-3
Allen, Shelton P.	Capt.	Regtl. Ammo Off.
Anderson, Ernie O.	1st Lt.	Co. A. C.O.
Anglim, Edward M.	Capt.	Co. L. C.O.
Babich, Peter C.	1st Lt.	Co. A.
Barker, Silas R.	1st Lt.	Co. K.
Battin, Donald H.	2nd Lt.	Co. E.
Becker, Philip A.	Capt.	Pers. Off.
Bemis, Russell B.	1st Lt.	Asst. Rgt. S-4
Berkowitz, Julius	Capt.	Rgt. Dent. Surg.
Blair, Oather	1st Lt.	D.S. Sixth Army
Bland, Irvin G.	1st Lt.	D.S. 24th Div.
Blaney, Kermit B.	1st Lt.	Co. L.
Bowman, Wheeler G.	2nd Lt.	Co. A.
Boyd, Wilbur B.	1st Lt.	Co. I.
Brown, Robert A.	Capt.	Hq. 1st Bn., Bn. S-1
Brown, Roy C.	1st Lt.	Co. G.
Browning, Newton F.	Capt.	Rgt. S-1
Bunkley, Thomas H.	2nd Lt.	Co. K.
Bussell, Frank T.	Major	Regt. S-4
Buttice, Angelo P.	2nd Lt.	Co. B.
Byrd, William M.	1st Lt.	Rgt. Com. Off.
Clifford, Thomas E. Jr.	Lt.Col.	Leave in U.S.
Coers, Burt N.	Major	Rgt. Surg.
Cooper, Clee S.	2nd Lt.	Co. F.
Corrigan, Michael J.	1st Lt.	Co. A.
Counts, Charles R.	1st Lt.	Co. C.
Courtney, Burl	2nd Lt.	Co. L.
Crosson, Hugh S. Jr.	Capt.	2nd Bn. Ex. Off.
Crouch, Theodore	1st Lt.	Co. B.
Curles, Cecil M.	1st Lt.	Cannon Co.
Dantzler, LeRoy A. Jr.	1st Lt.	D.S. 24th Div.
Dice, Francis R.	Major	2nd Bn. Bn. Comdr.
Didak, Eugene J.	2nd Lt.	Co. E.
Eastman, Walter R.	2nd Lt.	3rd Bn. Com. Off.
Eddy, Lowell P.	2nd Lt.	D.S. Sixth Army
Edleson, Harold	Capt.	Cannon Co. C.O.
Ender, Robert R.	1st Lt.	Co. H. C.O.
Evans, Roy A.	W.O.	Asst. Ammo. Off.
Farmer, Edward S.	1st Lt.	Co. D.
Farrell, John B.	1st Lt.	Hq. Co. 1st Bn.
Fisher, Francis R.	2nd Lt.	Co. E.
Ford, Clarence R.	2nd Lt.	Co. F.
Foster, Lute A. Jr.	2nd Lt.	Hq. Co. 1st Bn.
Fourqurean, Wade D.	1st Lt.	Co. A.
Gilbert, John T.	1st Lt.	Co. K.
Girardeau, John H. Jr.	Capt.	Leave in U.S.
Goldpaugh, John J.	1st Lt.	Leave in U.S.
Goean, Robert L.	Capt.	Hq. Co. 3rd Bn. C.O.
Gullie, Frank J.	W.O.	Asst. S-4
Haas, Arthur C.	1st Lt.	Co. H.

Halderson, Llewellyn D.	1st Lt.	Co. E.
Hall, Claude H.	1st Lt.	Co. F.
Haller, Robert F.	1st Lt.	Co. K.
Hammer, Richard P.	1st Lt.	Co. H.
Handel, David	1st Lt.	D.S. Hq. 24th Div.
Hansen, David W.	1st Lt.	Co. D.
Hartley, Russell W.	2nd Lt.	Co. B.
Hartman, Wm. H.	2nd Lt.	Co. B.
Hawkins, William S.	Capt.	3rd Bn. Surg.
Haywood, Major G.	1st Lt.	Sv. Co. MTO
Hudson, Roger W.	2nd Lt.	Hq. Co.
Hughes, William C. Jr.	1st Lt.	Co. A. C.O.
Irons, Philip S., III	1st Lt.	3rd Bn. S-3
Ivey, Paul B.	1st Lt.	2nd Bn. S-2
Jameson, Charles R. Jr.	Capt.	Co. F. C.O.
Johnson, Dale E.	1st Lt.	Co. I. C.O.
Jones, Erner	Capt.	2nd Bn. Surg.
Kelley, Jack H.	Capt.	Co. C. C.O.
Kester, Alfred J.	1st Lt.	Hq. Co. 3rd Bn.
Kilgo, Robert L.	1st Lt.	Co. E. C.O.
Lancaster, James L.	W.O.	Asst. Rgt. S-1
Langford, William N.	1st Lt.	Co. D.
Lannin, Thomas R.	1st Lt.	Hq. Co. 2nd Bn.
Leahy, John P.	Major	1st Bn. Bn. C.O.
Leatherman, Leland F.	Capt.	Rgt. S-2
Lemm, Stanley C.	1st Lt.	2nd Bn. S-4
Lesky, Albert W.	1st Lt.	2nd Bn. Asst. S-2
Little, Lamar W.	Major	3rd Bn. Bn. Exec.
Lockhart, Gerald L.	Capt.	Co. B. C.O.
Longridge, Kermit C.	1st Lt.	A.T. Co.
Luria, Sidney B.	1st Lt.	3rd Bn. Surg.
McFarland, James	1st Lt.	1st Bn. Com. Off.
McMaster, Rudolph J.	1st Lt.	Cannon Co.
Maclean, Ardell G.	1st Lt.	Co. C.
Madison, Seymour E.	Lt.Col.	Rgt. Exec.
Malone, Robert H.	1st Lt.	Co. C.
Marcy, Roy W.	Major	Leave in U.S.
Marks, Arthur	Capt.	1st Bn. Surg.
Marquez, Thomas	2nd Lt.	Co. G.
Mayer, John D.	1st Lt.	2nd Bn. S-3
Miller, George J.	1st Lt.	T.D. 19th Inf.
Moore, Dan. C.	1st Lt.	Co. H.
Morean, Gilbert W.	1st Lt.	A.T. Co.
Mote, Jack A.	1st Lt.	Hq. Co. 3rd Bn.
Murphy, James F.	1st Lt.	A.T. Co.
Nacheff, Steve P.	2nd Lt.	Rgt. Asst. S-4
Oler, William L.	1st Lt.	Leave in U.S.
Olson, Erwin L.	Capt.	Serv. Co. C.O.
Parent, James M.	1st Lt.	Co. F.
Patrick, Wm. J.	1st Lt.	3rd Bn. S-4
Pierce, James F.	1st Lt.	Co. K.
Postma, James L.	1st Lt.	3rd Bn. S-3
Prall, William A.	1st Lt.	Co. I.
Ramee, Eric P.	Lt.Col.	Hq. 3rd Bn. Bn. C.O.

Reid, Neil E.	Capt.	Co. M. C.O.
Rannaker, Evert D.	2nd Lt.	Co. I.
Rhein, William L.	1st Lt.	Asst. Dent. Surg.
Rogers, Edward J.	Capt.	Co. A. C.O.
Rogers, Woodrow W.	1st Lt.	Co. C.
Rosenblatt, Benjamin	2nd Lt.	Co. G.
Sabatine, Matthew	1st Lt.	Hq. Co. 1st Bn.
Sellmer, George	2nd Lt.	Co. M.
Seyle, Frank W.	1st Lt.	Hq. Co.
Sloan, Nicholas E.	Capt.	Rgt. S-3
Smigrod, Seymour	1st Lt.	Co. G.
Smith, Henry M.	1st Lt.	Rgt. Hq. Co. (I & R Plat)
Smith, Vinson S.	2nd Lt.	1st Bn. S-4
Stanford, Don D.	Capt.	3rd Bn. S-1
Steward, Alvin E.	1st Lt.	Co. F.
Suber, Tom W.	Capt.	Co. K. C.O.
Swast, John J.	Capt.	Co. D. C.O.
Thompson, James H.	Capt.	2nd Bn. S-1
Trembley, Arthur H. Jr.	1st Lt.	Co. D.
Ufer, Karl A.	Capt.	Regimental Chaplain
Upton, Sherwood A.	Capt.	Leave in U.S.
Vinneau, Ernest L.	1st Lt.	Co. K.
Walters, Murray M.	Capt.	Asst. Rgt. Chap.
Weber, Frederick R.	Lt.Col.	Rgt. Commander
Wheeler, Leroy C.	2nd Lt.	Co. M.
White, William C.	1st Lt.	Sv. Co. A&P Off.
Whitney, Charles R.	1st Lt.	Co. L.
Whitney, Howard H.	1st Lt.	Co. K.
Wicker, Glenes E.	1st Lt.	A.T. Co. C.O.
Wilson, Milton E.	1st Lt.	Co. K.
Wright, Albert J.	1st Lt.	Co. C.
Young, Emitte L.	1st Lt.	Hq. Co. 3rd Bn.

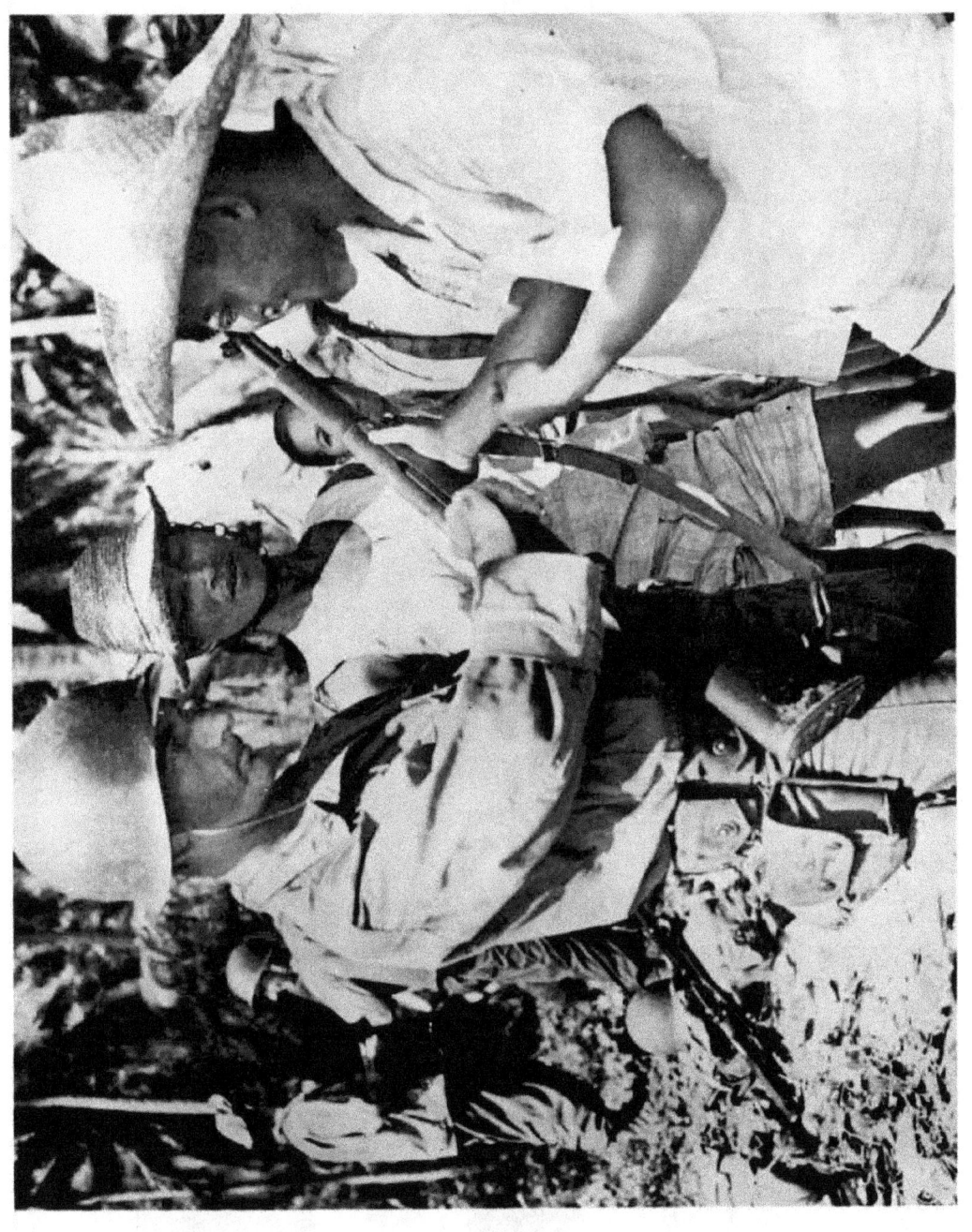

Private First Class William T. Little, King Company, shows his M-1 rifle to Filipinos, November 1944.

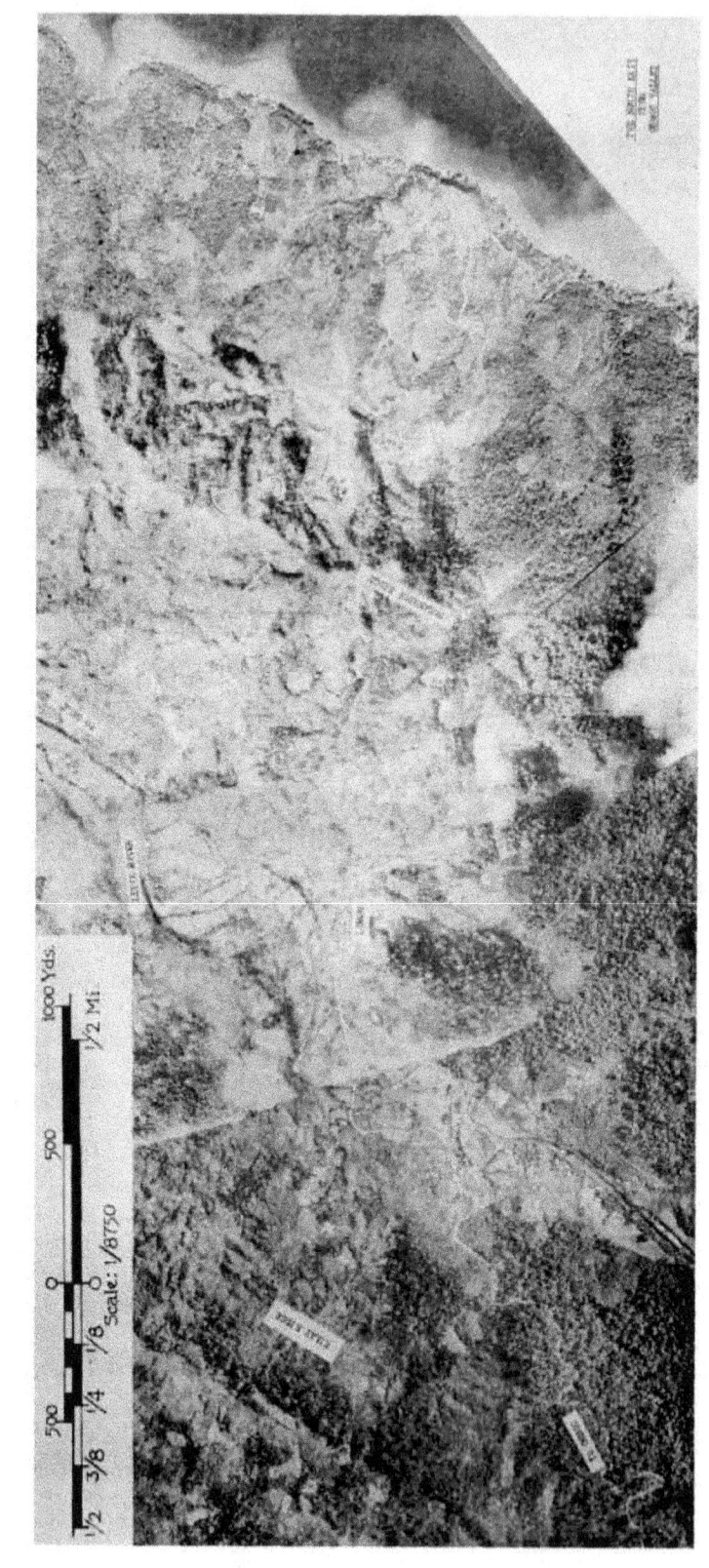

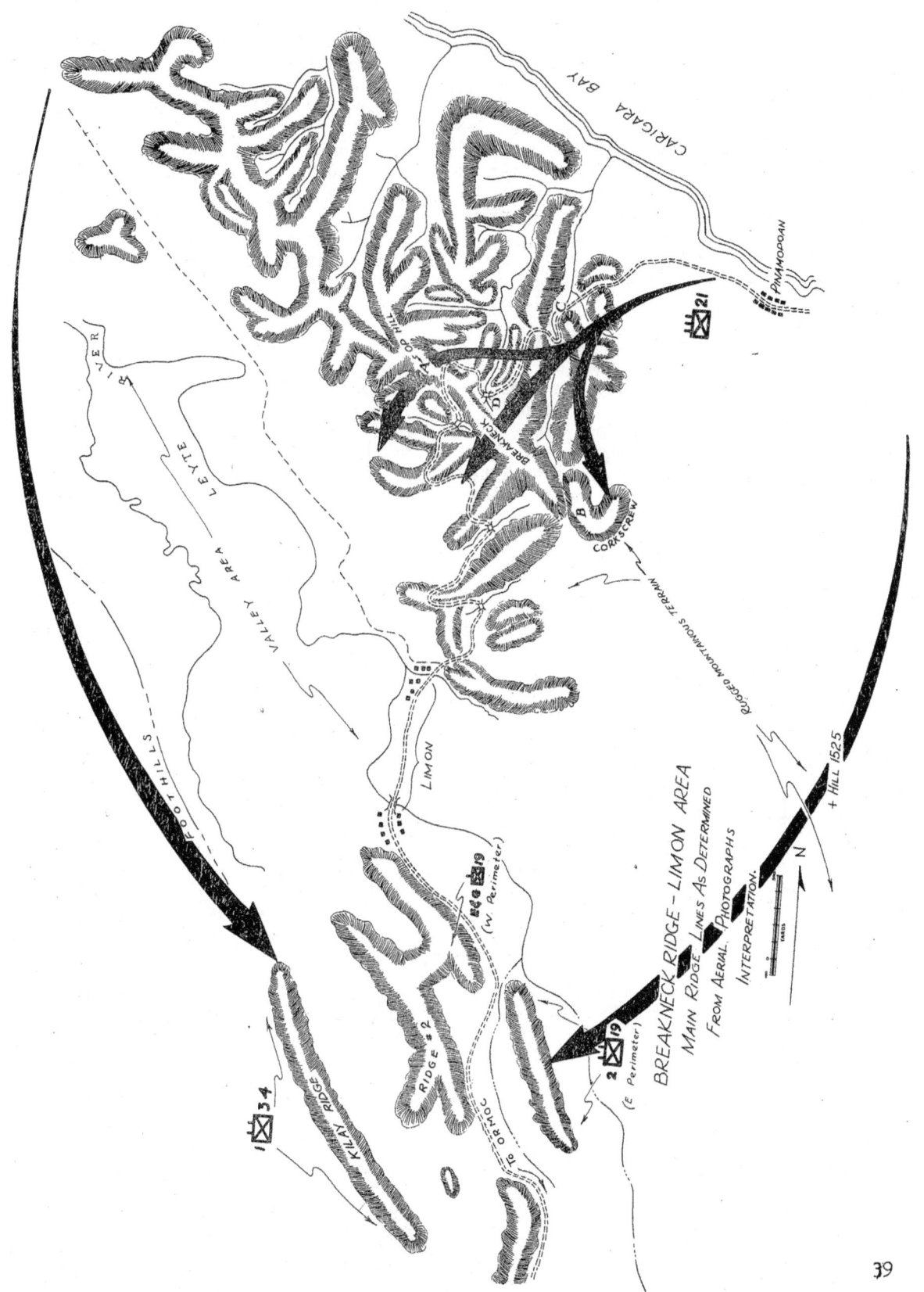

At the northern end of the Ormoc Valley on Leyte Island, the 21st Infantry fought and won one of the most bitterly contested battles of the war. Fighting centered around Breakneck Ridge, a deeply accented terrain feature. Breakneck Ridge is not a ridgeline, but is formed by a series of knobs. The low ground thick with shoulder high cogon grass, the pockets between the hills thickly wooded. The valleys are deep and precipitous. Even a small force ingeniously emplaced could have exacted enormous casualties. The seriousness of the task became apparent when the presence of the First Japanese Division was determined. The First Division, fresh from Manchuria, superbly trained and equipped, organized a system of trenches and interlocking pillboxes, varied to cover both surrounding trenches and prepared fields of fire. Heavily supported by 75mm, 105mm, and 150mm artillery, this crack combat unit had developed what they considered an invulnerable line.

During the 12 days from 5 November 1944 to 16 November 1944 (inclusive), a technique for clearing connecting trenches in terrain impassible for tanks, was perfected. Assault fire carried into a trench from which teams with grenades and tommy guns cleared the file from bend to bend. It was impossible to spot these fortifications because of the grass and excellent camouflage. Spider holes dug flush to the ground remained undiscovered even after troops had searched the area. Hundreds of these holes were scattered indiscriminately. Coordinated attack was difficult; movement limited by sniper fire and barely discernible automatic fields of fire.

Against this determined opposition an average of 200 yards a day was gained until the entire Breakneck Ridge was occupied. In the 2000 yard advance from the enemy's original front lines, 1,779 Japanese bodies had been counted. It is reasonable to assume many more lay dead in thick tropical vegetation. The action had been bitter for the 21st. Losses comprised heavy battle casualties and many from causes other then battle. Officer casualties were inordinately heavy. At the conclusion of the action, line companies averaged 1 officer and 85 enlisted men.

Difficulties arising from extremely broken terrain, sporadic communication, and inaccurate mapping were complicated by an intricate supply problem. Incessant rain transformed Leyte into one big mud hole. Carrying parties exhausted themselves carrying ammunition, water and rations. Rear echelon personnel were sent in and finally whole fighting units labored to supply the front lines. The men of the regiment were continually on the move, some fighting by day and hauling supplies by night. Aside from the discomfort and serious drop in efficiency under this rain, it provided a protective curtain during the day and covered the enemy's movements in night attacks. With Breakneck Ridge secured, the backbone of the island's resistance was broken. The successful termination of the action immeasurably hastened the end of Japanese occupation of Leyte.

By the time the 21st Infantry was committed, the enemy had completed its organized withdrawal from Pinamopoan and Carigara to the Breakneck Ridge area. Since the Ormoc Road runs through the ridge, this high ground takes on a definite importance.

The Jap First Division was a cocky outfit.

On November 4th the Regiment landed at Tanuan to meet the threat of newly landed Jap reinforcements. On the 5th the 21st Infantry Regimental combat team was trucked and marched rapidly across the Island to the vicinity of Pinamapoan on the North shore. In the days to follow the bloodiest battling of this war was to take place between Pinamapoan and Limon. The 21st Infantry met the enemy First Division, a force three times its size, head on. After a week of this fight while the 21st was still slugging forward, two arms reached out around our flanks and struck the Japanese near Limon. These daring flanking movements, although not a part of the Battle of Breakneck Ridge, described hereafter, deserve mention here. One Battalion of the Thirty-fourth Infantry under command of Lieut. Colonel Thomas Clifford (formerly of the 21st Infantry) took the right and one Battalion of the Nineteenth Infantry under command of Lieut. Colonel R. B. Spragins enveloped from the left. These two battalions made wide encirclements and were completely cut off from other troops and almost without lines of communications. This daring plan of Major General Fred Irving, Division Commander, was entirely unsuspected by the enemy. Both battalions fought desperately and gallantly. There is no doubt that the Japanese First Division was caught off balance and crippled by these two battalions.

This is a story of the 21st Infantry and the details of the fights of Clifford and Spragins will not be recounted here. However, the story of our successful action on Breakneck Ridge, in all probability, would never have been written had it not been for those two gallant battalions.

In the following account the actions of the Regiment are described in some detail. In reading it, one must remember that every move, every defense, every attack was closely supported by artillery. The division artillery of the 24th Division included three battalions of 105MM howitzers, the 13th, 52nd and 63rd Field Artillery Battalions and the 11th Field Artillery Battalion, 155MM howitzers. In addition to the constant and heavy supporting fire of this artillery, the X Corps artillery of one battalion each of 155MM howitzers, 155MM guns, and 8 inch howitzers fired day and night in our support.

BREAKNECK RIDGE OFFENSIVE

On the morning of 5 November 1944, the 21st Infantry was ordered to move to the PINAMOPOAN area and relieve the 34th Infantry. Dispositions of Battalions at 0600, 5 November 1944 were as follows: 3rd Battalion and Headquarters Company were in the vicinity of COLASION: 1st Battalion at vicinity of CAPOOCAN, 2nd Battalion and Separate Units had just arrived at TANUAN and were preparing to move to vicinity of TUNGA. At approximately 0930, 5 November 1944, a meeting was held at the 34th Infantry CP at PINAMOPOAN. Officers attending from the 21st Infantry were the Regimental Commander, Executive Officer, 3rd Battalion Commander, S-2, S-3, and 3rd Battalion S-3. General plan of relief which was agreed upon was as follows: 3rd Battalion, 21st Infantry to have road priority and move directly up Highway #2 and relieve 3rd Battalion 34th Infantry as soon as possible. Upon arrival in that area by 3rd Battalion 21st Infantry the 3rd Battalion 34th Infantry was to immediately move to the rear with priority on road. Approximate location of the 3rd Battalion 34th Infantry at the time of relief was (07.1-68.0). 1st Battalion 21st Infantry was to move up after the 3rd Battalion, 34th Infantry had cleared, and occupy the area held by 2nd Battalion, 34th Infantry in the vicinity of (07.5-68.2)

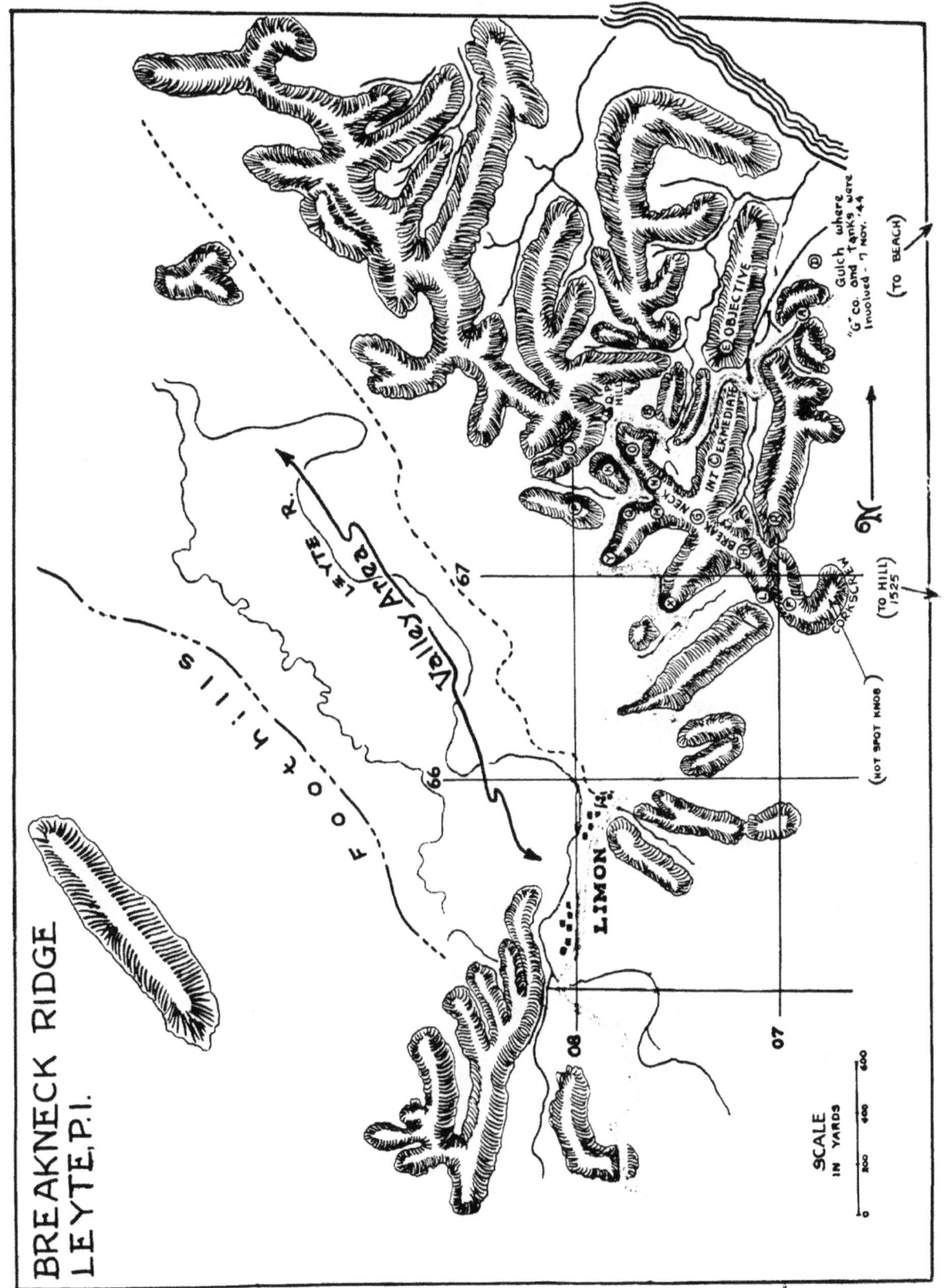

From approximately 1000-1115, the Regimental Commander, Lieut. Col. Frederick Weber, 3rd Battalion Commander, Lt.Col. Eric Ramee, and Regimental S-3, Capt. Nicholas Sloan, made reconnaissance of the area to place the two Battalions. At the 3rd Battalion, 34th Infantry CP, the Executive Officer, 34th Infantry joined the Reconnaissance party. The Regimental Commander decided to make a reconnaissance for the 1st Battalion, and the 3rd Battalion Commander, Regimental S-3 with the Executive Officer, 34th Infantry as a guide were to look over the forward area. It was soon discovered that the highest and most commanding ground in the area hadn't been occupied so the 3rd Battalion Commander decided to occupy it upon arrival of his Battalion. The party picked up a squad from Company "E", 34th Infantry at Point "A" and proceeded towards the bridge. Men from this squad were dropped off at intervals to the east of the road to occupy the high ground (Point "C"), thus providing local security for the Reconnaissance Party. At the bridge two jeeps from the 52nd Field Artillery Battalion were parked and drivers said that the officers and a forward observer party were on the high ground conducting fire at a school house that had 25 Japs in it. The Executive Officer, 34th Infantry confirmed this. The Reconnaissance party proceeded from the bridge forward to Point "B", without security as the squad was all disposed. At the furthermost point that the Reconnaissance party had advanced they could see the target that the Artillery was firing on. The target was about 300 yards on up the road. At this point the Reconnaissance party came back to the bridge and worked their way up to the high ground on the east side of the road at Point "C". From this high ground, the Artillery firing on OP hill was observed. No contact was ever made with men from Company "K" who were sent up from the road to occupy this ground while the party made its reconnaissance up the road. At approximately 1115, the 3rd Battalion Commander left to meet his Battalion. The Regimental S-3 met the Regimental Commander and returned. While enroute back to the CP a reconnaissance was made for the Regimental CP. A site at Point "A" was selected. At 1230, upon return of the Regimental Commander and the S-3 to the Regimental CP, the Regimental Executive Officer had a message from the artillery that their forward OP was being attacked. A message was sent to the 3rd Battalion Commander at 1240 to investigate and take necessary action. At 1330, the 3rd Battalion Commander requested the artillery to cease firing. This fire soon ceased.

Later on in the afternoon of 5 November 1944, it was learned that Company "K" had occupied OP Hill with slight opposition and had freed the 52nd Field Artillery party. Company "I" had occupied the high ground later named "Hot Spot Knob". Both companies dug in. The 3rd Battalion attempted to run ammunition, food and shovels to "I" & "K" Companies but enemy fire prevented this. Small amounts of ammunition reached "K" Company. Meanwhile the 1st Battalion moved to the vicinity of PINAMOPOAN. "A" and "B" Companies then moved to areas occupied by 2nd Battalion, 34th Infantry. Company "C" remained in the vicinity of COLASION to guard bridges. By dark, troop dispositions were as follows: Company "I" and Heavy Machine Gun Section, "Hot Spot Knob"; Company "K" and Heavy Machine Gun Section, O.P. Hill; Company "L" as follows: 1 platoon as litter bearers and carrying parties; 1 platoon for Battalion CP defense, 1 platoon with Company "K". During the night both Company "I" and "K" were counterattacked. The 3rd Battalion, 19th Infantry

BRONZE STAR

Captain TOM W. SUBER, Infantry, U. S. Army. For heroic achievement in connection with military operations against the enemy near PASSANGRAHN, DUTCH NEW GUINEA, from 29 April to 3 May 1944. When two patrols of an infantry regiment were ambushed and pinned down by intense enemy machine gun fire, Captain Suber immediately organized and personally led another platoon to the scene. Due to his excellent leadership, initiative and good judgment, the enemy was taken by surprise and quickly fled, thus relieving the beleagured patrols. Throughout this entire period Captain Suber displayed a high degree of initiative and leadership, quickly establishing control of his men after landing, and maintaining excellent control and order during the advance to HOLLANDIA DROME, in spite of tremendous supply and evacuation difficulties. Captain Suber's unselfish devotion to duty during this entire period reflects great credit upon himself and the military service.

SILVER STAR (POSTHUMOUS)

Staff Sergeant ANTONIO PEPE, Infantry, United States Army. For gallantry in action near Pinamopoan, Leyte, Philippine Islands, on 6 November 1944. Sergeant Pepe volunteered to go to the rear to bring up vitally needed machine gun and mortar ammunition. With utter disregard for his own safety he crossed ground in a truck under intense enemy fire. Upon returning with ammunition the truck was hit, putting it out of action. Sergeant Pepe jumped out of the truck and assisted in the defense of this ammunition securing it until elements of his unit were able to reach it. He gave his life for this cause. Sergeant Pepe's courage and determination are a credit to himself and are in accord with the highest traditions of the service.

SILVER STAR

Staff Sergeant (then Sergeant) DOMINIC R. CASTRO, Infantry, United States Army. For gallantry in action at Breakneck Ridge, Leyte, Philippine Islands, on 6 November 1944. Sergeant Castro was a squad leader in an infantry rifle company. The enemy made a bayonet charge on his position. Sergeant Castro was hit by a grenade and also bayoneted. He stayed in his position without medical attention until he was properly relieved. By his remaining in position, enemy infiltration was not possible. Sergeant Castro displayed true devotion to duty and was an inspiration to all who witnessed his actions.

SILVER STAR

Private CHARLES E. CLEMMER, Infantry, United States Army. For gallantry in action at Breakneck Ridge, Leyte, Philippine Islands, on 5 November 1944. Private Clemmer was an automatic rifleman in an infantry company. During a heavy attack against the enemy he was on the left flank of his platoon. In this action the squad leader and several of the men were killed One enemy soldier threw a grenade at Private Clemmer's BAR and he caught the grenade in one hand and threw it back thus saving the lives of the BAR team. Private Clemmer's quick thinking and complete disregard for his own personal safety was a source of inspiration to all who witnessed his actions and reflects great credit upon himself and the military service.

SILVER STAR

Staff Sergeant (then Private First Class) ANTHONY J. JASIUIEWIEZ, Infantry, United States Army. For gallantry in action at Leyte, Philippine Islands, on 5 November 1944. Sergeant Jasiukiewiez was a scout for an infantry rifle platoon. He pushed forward in front of his platoon under heavy enemy fire and covered a trail to prevent an enemy flanking movement while his platoon moved into position. Later in the same action, he volunteered and went on three patrols into enemy territory and brought back valuable information concerning enemy strength and dispositions. Throughout the whole action, he demonstrated a high degree of personal courage and disregard for his safety and was an inspiration to all the men of his platoon. His action reflects great credit upon himself and the military service.

SILVER STAR

Private MELVIN L. TAYLOR, Infantry, United States Army. For gallantry in action at Leyte, Philippine Islands, on 6 November 1944. Private Taylor volunteered to go to the rear to bring up vitally needed machine gun and mortar ammunition. With utter disregard for his own safety he crossed ground in a truck under intense enemy fire. Upon returning with ammunition the truck was hit putting it out of action. Private Taylor jumped from the truck and assisted in the defense of this ammunition securing it until elements of his unit were able to reach it. Private Taylor's courage and determination are a credit to himself and are in accord with the highest traditions of the military service.

SILVER STAR

Major (then Captain) TOM W. SUBER, Infantry, United States Army. For gallantry in action in the Philippine Islands, on 5 and 6 November 1944. About noon, on 5 November, a group of artillery observers were beseiged by the enemy at an observation post situated on a ridge. As commanding officer of the advance guard company of an infantry battalion, Captain Suber led the attack against the enemy, personally participating with the assault elements. His prompt and energetic action and his fearless leadership undoubtedly saved the lives of the artillery observers. Captain Suber's company occupied and organized the defense of the ridge. The enemy attacked the company's perimeter once during the day, and three times during the night. Due to his organizational ability and his timely use of counter-attack, his company succeeded in repelling the enemy attacks. The perimeter was subjected to almost continual fire by enemy automatic weapons, knee mortars, and artillery. Despite the enemy fire, Captain Suber exposed himself time after time observing the situation and visiting and encouraging his men. Captain Suber's courage was a source of inspiration to all members of his command and reflects great credit upon himself and the military service.

BRONZE STAR

Private First Class GEORGE L. JESTER, Infantry, United States Army. For heroic achievement in connection with military operations against the enemy at Pinamopoan Pass, Leyte, Philippine Islands, on 6 November 1944. Private Jester was an acting squad leader of a mortar squad in an infantry rifle company. His great vigor and leadership in controlling his men when they were subject to heavy mortar and machine gun fire from the enemy, saved not only the men under his control, but also valuable equipment. His coolness and courage were an inspiration to his unit and reflect credit upon himself and the military service.

BRONZE STAR

Private First Class ROBERT B. MILLER, Infantry, United States Army. For heroic achievement in connection with military operations against the enemy at Leyte, Philippine Islands, on 5 November 1944. Private Miller was a rifleman in an infantry rifle company. During a heavy attack and under continuous enemy fire he evacuated several wounded men who otherwise would have died. He brought up much needed ammunition and acted as a runner for the platoon. He later directed fire on a trail on which the enemy was bringing up reinforcements, and caused heavy casualties among the enemy. Private Miller's total disregard for his own personal safety was a source of inspiration to all who witnessed his actions and reflects great credit upon himself and the military service.

A GI drags a dead Jap out of a pillbox. But the Jap had got some Yanks before.

SILVER STAR

Second Lieutenant (then Technical Sergeant) ANDREW E. PRISTAS, Infantry, United States Army. For gallantry in action near Pinamopoan, Leyte, Philippine Islands, on 5-6 November 1944. On 5 November 1944 Sergeant Pristas was commanding a platoon of heavy .30 caliber machine guns, when two companies of the battalion were cut off by the enemy. In the face of enemy fire and with complete disregard for his own personal safety, Sergeant Pristas went from machine gun to machine gun of his platoon checking ammunition and targets, and instilling confidence in his men. When the withdrawal was ordered after three enemy attacks on the night of 5-6 November 1944, he remained behind with one section of his machine guns to cover the withdrawal of his company, firing upon the advancing enemy for fully one half hour and successfully carrying out his mission. His outstanding courage and devotion to duty in the face of enemy fire is worty of the highest traditions of the military service.

BRONZE STAR (Posthumous)

First Lieutenant LLEWELLYN D. HALDERSON, Infantry, United States Army. For heroic achievement in connection with military operations against the enemy near ***** ***** on 6 November 1944. Lieutenant Halderson was a rifle platoon leader when the perimeter of his company was attacked by an estimated company of the enemy. In the face of enemy rifle, machine gun and mortar fire, Lieutenant Halderson checked his part of the perimeter and found a gap created by several casualties. Under enemy fire he crossed the area, secured reinforcements and a box of grenades, returned and successfully filled the gap and prevented a break-through by the enemy. He found one of his men lying wounded nearby and assisted him back to the center of the perimeter where he received medical attention. Lieutenant Halderson's undaunted courage and devotion to duty reflect great credit upon himself and the military service.

Mail for the Gimlets, 4 November 1944 on Leyte.

took over beach defense in PINAMOPOAN sector and established strong outposts to the South of Highway #2 before dark.

Plan of attack for the following day. Companies "I" and "K" to clear ridge assisted by Company "A" attacking up the road. Company "G" to follow and be prepared to make reconnaissance of area South of LIMON and MOUNT CATABARAN. At 2100, the S-3 met advance party from 2nd Battalion at CAPOOCAN and made reconnaissance of Bivouac area in the vicinity of COLASION. 2nd Battalion closed in Bivouac area at 2345. The Third Battalion was attacked all night by strong enemy forces and were under heavy artillery concentrations.

There was no map whatsoever of the terrain except a radically inaccurate map of Leyte Island which was 1/250,000 scale. This condition was true for the next twelve days.

6 November 1944: 3rd Battalion units were completely cut off and under violent attack. Company "A" jumped off at 0800, from vicinity of 3rd Battalion CP (Point "D") to advance to vicinity of bridge. At 1155 stiff opposition drove Company "A" to the rear. Casualties were high especially among officers. At 0920, the first message came from Company "I" on "Hot Spot Knob" stating they saw 20 Japanese retreating towards LIMON. At 0925 Company "C" reinforced with Filipino scouts left to occupy Hill 1525 which overlooks 3rd Battalion defensive area. At 1140, report that snipers were working in towards Company "B" who sent a patrol out to intercept. At approximately 1300, the Third Battalion withdrew to the vicinity of the beach. Meanwhile 2nd Battalion and elements of the 3rd Battalion were reorganizing and defending line along former 3rd Battalion CP. (Points "A" and "D"). 3rd Battalion assembled and reorganized in the vicinity of PINAMOPOAN. During the night of 6 to 7 November 1944, 2nd Battalion CP was counterattacked. Company "C" returned at approximately 1710, and reported no contacts but that the guides and scouts had become lost and brought them back.

7 November 1944: 2nd Battalion jumped off at 0800. Company "E" was on right of road and reached intermediate objective with small opposition. Company "G" on left of road ran into trouble in bottom of gulch prior to reaching intermediate objective. Tank destroyers were used to fire direct fire into pocket. Tanks were sent down road and before reaching the bridge, one tank was knocked out by a Japanese who placed a land mine on it. Company "L" was ordered to take intermediate objective on left of road by wide encircling movement to the left. Company "L" failed to reach objective by dark and withdrew, and set up perimeter with Company "F", on left flank of intermediate objective.

The following summary for the period above is taken from Headquarters X Corps weekly report No. 3, for the week ending 11 November 1944.

"No outstanding activity until evening of 5 November 1944. By evening the 3rd Battalion, 21st Infantry, occupied the high ground 1000- 1500 yards south of PINAMOPOAN and were in contact with an estimated 300 Japanese."

"6 November 1944, the Japanese succeeded in driving the 21st Infantry from the ridge and by night had dug in on the Northwest slopes of the ridge and harassed our forward elements with mortar, and 75mm Artillery Fire in addition to several piecemeal attacks during the night, one of which resulted in the death of 18 Japanese, including a Captain, two Lieutenants. By evening a patrol from the 21st Infantry, had reached Hill 1525 and had made no contacts."

"7 November 1944, the leading Battalion 21st Infantry made contact with the forward elements of an estimated enemy battalion on a general line from (06.6-67.0) to (07.5-66.5). The enemy well dug in and delayed their advance with small arms, automatic weapons, mortars, and a battery of artillery. Several pockets of resistance were cleaned out during the day but the enemy resisted stubbornly, from well dug in positions on commanding terrain. Company "G" 19th Infantry upon occupation of Hill 1525 at 1700 discovered a Japanese perimeter of unknown strength on the South Slope". (It was later known that Company "G", 19th Infantry was not on Hill 1525 but was one or two miles to the east thereof.)

        Casualties for 21st Infantry, 5, 6, and 7 November 1944.
        40 Killed in Action, 117 Wounded, and 3 Missing.

Extract from Headquarters X Corps Weekly Report No. 3, for week ending 11 November 1944.

"The enemy's operations plan as of 6 November 1944 envisiaged the 57th 49th and 41st Regiments disposed from left to right on the semi-circular and ridged high ground running generally Southeast from a point Southwest of PINAMOPOAN - - - that dog tags, pay books, and other identifications taken from enemy dead indicate that enemy units are in and disposed in accordance with proposed plan of operations disclosed in captured map of 6 November 1944."

At dawn 7 November 1944, Regimental Field Order #19, was distributed to units concerned. Extracts there from as follows:

1.   a. Enemy, strength undetermined, holds high ground on ridge 400 yards South of 2nd Battalion. Elements of the 1st Japanese Division, remanents of the 16th Division in foothills and mountains South of line CARIGARA - PINAMOPOAN.

    b. Division artillery supports attack with 15 minutes preparation from 0750 to 0805 on intermediate objective. Further fire on call.

2. 21st Infantry resumes attack South astride PINAMOPOAN - ORMOC ROAD. Time of attack 0800, 7 November 1944. Formation: Column of Battalions, 2nd, 1st, 3rd. Line of Departure: Present front lines.

3.   a. 2nd Battalion 21st Infantry:
      (1) Initial objective: Ridge 400 yards South of Present Front Lines.
      (2) First objective: Seize and secure high ground (see opns sketch).
      (3) Will patrol from first objective.

    b. 1st Battalion initially Regimental Reserve - present positions will be prepared to move on order.

c. 3rd Battalion initially Regimental Reserve - present positions will be prepared to move on order.

d. 52nd Field Artillery will mass its fires on intermediate objective from 0750-0805, then lift to first objective. Thereafter fires on call.

e. 1st Platoon, Company "A", 44th Tank Battalion will be prepared to support 2nd Battalion.

f. Company "C" 85th Chemical Battalion will reconnoiter for positions to support attack on first objective.

g. 3rd Battalion, 19th Infantry (attached), secures PINAMOPOAN area.

h. 1st Platoon, Company "A", 3rd Engineers continues with present mission.

i. Company "C" 632nd Tank Destroyer Battalion upon arrival will reconnoiter for positions to support attack of 2nd Battalion.

j. 7th Portable Surgical Hospital continues with present mission.

In this attack as stated above, Company "E" alone advanced 250 yards and took the hill to their immediate front (North of the road and right flank of the assigned "intermediate objective".) There they held the ground for the remainder of the day and that night, although there was a strongly held pocket of resistance on their left (South) which was not taken. Company "G" and the tanks were held by this pocket and failed to gain its intermediate objective. Company "L" was then ordered to make an encirclement to the left and take the portion of the intermediate objective on the left of the road. This attack failed. It withdrew to the southwest and joined Company "F" which had advanced about 400 yards and then withdrew due to a misunderstanding of orders. Company "F" when joined by Company "L" was on the near slope of the hill assigned as the intermediate objective for the day.

At noon 7 November 1944, Colonel W. J. Verbeck assumed command of the regiment.

Service and supply echelons which were far in rear (TUNGA) at the beginning of the operation were just now appearing. Rations and ammunition supply presented the greatest difficulties and supply functioning (only moved by carrying parties) were very inadequate.

At 15:45, 7 November 1944, Lieutenant Colonel Madison, formerly Regimental Executive Officer assumed command of the 2nd Battalion. The former Regimental Commander was appointed Regimental Executive Officer. All positions consolidated and units reorganized.

At 2000, 7 November 1944 - Field Order #20 was issued, Extracts therefrom as follows:

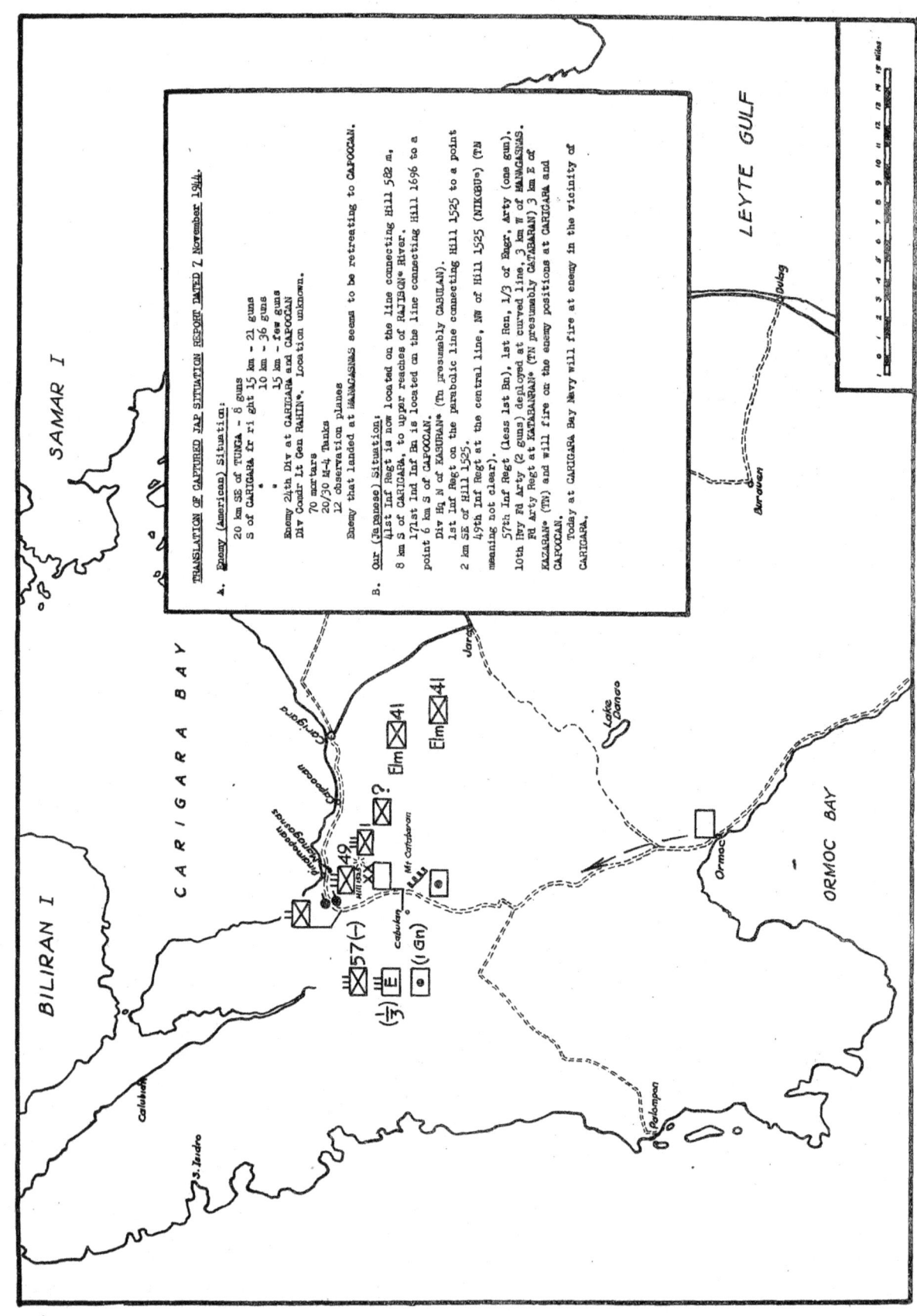

1. a. Enemy resistance of unknown strength is located in the ravine along the road at (07.5-67.0) and is dug into the hillside on both sides of the road. Occupied defensive installations are also located on high ground at (07.0-66.1) and (09.2-63.8)

    b. Division and corps artillery is sited for close support of operation.

2. This Regiment will attack South, 0700, 8 November 1944 with two battalions in assault. 2nd Battalion with Company "L" attached on the right; 1st Battalion on the left; by an initial frontal attack and wide envelopment of enemy's right to destroy enemy forces delaying along highway 2.

3. a. 2nd Battalion Company "L" attached will attack to capture high ground to the South at 0700. From there this Battalion will attack southward to secure the ridges (06.5-66.2)-(07.2-66.0)-(08.3-66.0).
    b. 1st Battalion with Intelligence and Reconnaissance Platoon attached will, from its present position envelop the enemy right flank, occupy Hill 1525 (3000 yards to Southeast) and will be prepared to continue attack on Highway 2 when ordered.

The 3rd Battalion was held in Regimental reserve and all attached units were assigned supporting missions. A 10 minute artillery preparation was to proceed the attack of the 2nd Battalion.

At 0700 the 2nd Battalion jumped off and attacked objectives and the pocket of resistance along the road. Flame throwers were employed to good advantage. Enemy artillery was active, shelling the road, the bridge at the bottom of the gulch and ranging in near Regimental C.P. at 0840 Company "F" reported from intermediate objective that it was moving forward to secure the high ground on the final objective.

At 1700, 7 November the Regimental Intelligence and Reconnaissance Platoon was attached to the 1st Battalion for the purpose of recohnoitering a route to Hill 1525 the next day. The 1st Battalion started on its wide encircling move at 0700, 8 November 1944 and moved towards Hill 1525. Information was received from Division that the 2nd Battalion, 19th Infantry had been ordered to move and to hold 1525, so the 1st Battalion had been ordered to move from that hill on an azmuth of 280 degrees to cut ORMOC road about 1800 yards south of LIMON to prevent the escape of the enemy from PINAMOPOAN Ridge Line.

At 0832, 8 November 1944 message received from 2nd Battalion, 19th Infantry that they were on high ground near Hill 1525 but had not secured good observation. (it later proved that this Battalion had taken the wrong ridge to the South from the beach and were from two to three miles to the Northwest of Hill 1525.)

At 1600, the 1st Battalion reported being on the South Slopes of Hill 1525, and was in contact with a force of enemy armed with automatic weapons, and mortars on the North and Northwest slopes of the same hill.

Nothing further was heard from 2nd Battalion, 19th Infantry.

Twenty-first Infantrymen examining Jap Artillery Piece on Leyte, November 1944.

C-47, dropping ammunition by parachute to 21st Infantry troops on Breakneck Ridge, November 12, 1944.

Major General Fred A. Irving, C. G. 24th Division, Brig. Gen. Ken C. Cramer, Assistant Division Commander and Lieutenant Page observe results of attack of the 21st Infantry at Breakneck Ridge, Leyte, November 13, 1944.

Lieut. Col. Lamar W. Little, C.O. 1st Battalion at Breakneck Ridge

The Late Captain Jack Kelley
C.O. Co. G, Later Executive
Officer 2nd Battalion

Capt. R. L. Kilgo
C.O. Company E

Major James H. Thompson
2nd Battalion

Capt. John D. (Red) Mayer
S-3, 2nd Battalion

Lt. Leroy Dantzler Jr.
First Battalion and Anti Tank Company

Lt. Andrew E. Pristas
Promoted in Mike
Company for Gallantry

Capt. M. D. Aitken
Hq. First Battalion

Capt. Claude E. Hall
Formerly 1st Lieut. Co. C,
Twice Wounded Philippines

SILVER STAR (Posthumous)

Sergeant FRANCIS E. HOGG, Field Artillery, United States Army. For gallantry in action against the enemy near Limon, Leyte, Philippine Islands, 8 November 1944. Sergeant Hogg, a radio operator with an artillery forward observer party attached to a company of infantry which had been assigned the mission of guarding our extremely important left flank against repeated strong enemy attacks, displayed extraordinary heroism in attempting to attend a radio from another field artillery battalion which he realized would have made possible the furnishing of additional artillery support to our infantry. Despite the heavy enemy fire which had wounded the forward observer in his party and all members of the only other field artillery party present, and with utter disregard for his own safety, he rushed from his foxhole to retrieve a temporarily abandoned radio from the other artillery battalion upon being told the infantry needed additional artillery support. He had barely cleared his foxhole when he was killed by enemy fire. Up to the time he was fatally wounded he performed his duties in an outstanding manner and contributed greatly toward breaking up repeated enemy attacks and in saving our troops many casualties. Sergeant Hogg's unselfish and outstanding act of heroism and his exemplary devotion to duty were an inspiration to all those with whom he worked and reflect great credit upon himself and the military service.

SILVER STAR

First Lieutenant LESTER B. KING, Field Artillery, United States Army. For gallantry in action near Pinamopoan, Leyte, Philippine Islands, during the period 8 and 9 November 1944. Lieutenant King was assigned as artillery forward observer with a company of infantry which had been assigned the mission of guarding the extremely important left flank of our lines. Shortly before noon on 8 November the enemy began launching a series of determined attacks in an attempt to dislodge the company from its commanding position. During one of these attacks around 1200 on 8 November, Lieutenant King became badly wounded in the arm and hand by machine gun fire. Knowing that the hard-pressed company greatly depended on him for artillery support and realizing the extremely urgent need for such support, he refused to leave his post of duty although in great pain from his wounds. For twenty-four hours under heavy fire and with no medical attention except first aid, he brough effective artillery fire on one enemy attack after another until the enemy advance had been stopped and reinforcements could be sent up to help the company out of its difficult situation. By his great skill and heroic conduct, he was to an outstanding degree responsible for breaking up the repeated enemy attacks and for thus permitting the company to hold our left flank intact until a counterattack could be organized to drive the enemy back.

SILVER STAR

Technical Sergeant WILLIAM SCRAPPER, JR., Infantry, United States Army. For gallantry in action at Leyte, Philippine Islands, on 9 November 1944. On this day, an infantry battalion attacked and seized a hill. After the hill was seized, the enemy counter attacked fiercely. During this enemy counter attack, Sergeant Scrapper was the platoon sergeant of a heavy weapons platoon. While inspecting his heavy machine gun positions, he discovered that the crew of one of his heavy guns had been put out of action by enemy fire. Sergeant Scrapper realizing that the fire of the machine gun was necessary in aiding to repulse the enemy counter attack, alone set up the machine gun again and made it ready for firing. He then took the position of gunner, and resumed fire upon the enemy. He performed all the functions of the members of the gun crew, and succeeded in maintaining fire upon the enemy until the counter attack was repulsed. The fire from Sergeant Scrapper's machine gun contributed materially to repulsing the counter attack of a determined enemy. Sergeant Scrapper's daring and fearless display of courage was a source of inspiration to all who witnessed his actions, and reflects great credit upon himself and the military service.

SILVER STAR

Captain CHARLES R. JAMESON, Infantry, United States Army. For gallantry in action at Pinamopoan, Leyte, Phillipine Islands, from 8 November to 15 November 1944. During this period, Captain Jameson displayed leadership and personal courage of the highest order. On 8 November, he led the successful attack on "Hot Spot Knob", a part of Breakneck Ridge, consolidating the position and coordinating its defense for the next six days. Countless times during this period, Captain Jameson exposed himself to the fire from enemy positions, some only fifty yards distant, to visit outlying parts of the perimeter and to act as observer for artillery and mortar fire. On 10 November, he extricated a platoon from a position in which they were receiving flanking fire on both sides. He was the last man to withdraw. On 11 November, he stood up in the face of a vicious enemy attack where the enemy automatic fire was inflicting heavy damage, and shouted: "Get up and return the fire! They are not shooting at you, they're shooting at me!" On 15 November, his personal daring and leadership were largely responsible for the knocking out and capturing of five Japanese light machine guns. Captain Jameson's courageous actions reflect great credit upon himself and the military service.

SILVER STAR

Staff Sergeant (then Sergeant) LOUIS G. KEPLER, Infantry, United States Army. For gallantry in action at Breakneck Ridge, Leyte, Philippine Islands, on 10 November 1944. Sergeant Kepler was a squad leader of a light machine gun section of an infantry rifle company. During the withdrawal of the company, which his squad was covering, he succeeded in crawling to his gun and destroying it when further action against the enemy could not be taken. The men in Sergeant Kepler's squad had all been killed or wounded by extremely heavy enemy machine gun and mortar fire, which continued throughout the time he was destroying his machine gun. Once the gun was put out of action, he assisted in removing the wounded to safety. His outstanding bravery in this instance is notable and reflects high credit upon himself and the military service.

At dark 8 November 1944 the units of the 21st Infantry were disposed as follows:

1st Battalion on South Slopes of Hill 1525.

Company "F" at Point "F" on BREAKNECK RIDGE its final objective for the day and was in contact with strong hostile forces to its South and East.

Company "E" at at Point "E" on its intermediate objective.

The Bridge on the ORMOC ROAD between Points "B" and "C" had been destroyed by the enemy. This cut the only route of approach to OP Hill to Tanks and Tank Destroyers.

Enemy emplacements flanking this bridge with rifle, automatic weapons, mortar and artillery fire were holding Company "E" in place.

Company "L" at "Point "C" had not advanced but had been subjected to infiltrating attacks by enemy infantry throughout the afternoon. At 1530 the last enemy attack against Company "L" had failed.

Artillery fire of 15 centimeter caliber was now being received in the area of "the intermediate objective" and the Regiments rear elements. Overs from this fire were hitting in the bay to the North.

Throughout the day the enemy had continued to stubbornly resist the advance of all elements, sniper fire was continuous in front, flanks and rear of all positions. 43 Japanese bodies were counted within our position.

The enemy capabilities at the close of 8 November 1944 as enumerated by G-2, 24th Division were as follows:

    a. Offensive action towards PINAMOPOAN by enemy forces moving North from ORMOC.
    b. Offensive action North toward PINAMOPOAN combined with flanking effort in direction of JARO over TAMBUCO - JARO trail (6 miles to Southeast).
    c. Infiltration to our rear areas to disrupt our lines of communications and harass our Perimeters."

The 21st Infantry was ordered by Commanding General, 24th Division at 1000, 8 November to maintain the initiative at all costs.

The 24th Division Field Order 9 November 1944 is quoted in part as follows:

"3a. 21st Infantry will:
    (1) Attack and capture Division objective (Ridge Line 4000 yards South of LIMON).
    (2) Upon capture of Division objective, patrol vigorously to the South and prepare to continue attack towards ORMOC.
    (3) Will protect West flank of Corps. The zone of action of the 21st Infantry was approximately 4,000 yards.

ACTION OF THE 1ST BATTALION, 21ST INFANTRY, 9 November 1944.

There was heavy rain all day reaching Typhoon proportions by 1430. The 1st Battalion at dawn, leaving Company "A" to hold Hill 1525 until the early expected arrival of the 2nd Battalion, 19th Infantry moved on an azmuth of 280 degrees towards the ORMOC road South of LIMON carrying out their order to make the wide envelopment of the enemy's right.

At 0950 the 1st Battalion less Company "A" had proceeded generally West for approximately one and one half miles and reported they were held upon the slopes of a hill within sight of the ORMOC Road by heavy enemy fire and were being attacked from front and both flanks.

At 1140, 1st Battalion had moved to the Northwest slowly and was less than a mile East of LIMON.

No word had been received from 2nd Battalion, 19th Infantry but it was assumed that the Battalion was moving towards Hill 1525.

At 1150, Company "A" on Hill 1525 was being hard pressed to hold the position against heavy enemy frontal and flank attacks. The First Battalion commander was ordered to withdraw to Hill 1525 with the remainder of the Battalion and hold that hill.

At 1250 withdrawal was complete and Battalion Commander reported he was being attacked by strong enemy forces on three sides. He reported his losses were heavy.

The Regimental Commander reported to division that no sign of the 2nd Battalion 19th Infantry had been noted, and 1st Battalion was hard pressed on Hill 1525; at 1400, 1st Battalion Commander reported that he had retreated from Hill 1525, and was using Company "A" as a covering force for the withdrawal. At 1830, 1st Battalion had withdrawn 3500 yards to the North and had formed a perimeter for the night South of the Beach, East of PINAMOPOAN.

The 2nd Battalion, 19th Infantry had confused directions and guides from another organization had misled them. They were in fact 3000-4000 yards to the Northeast of 1525 in very rough wooded and hilly country.

ACTION OF 21ST INFANTRY, LESS 1ST BATTALION, 9 November 1944.

The Regiment was ordered to attack astride the ORMOC Road with the 2nd Battalion (Less Company "F") on the right of the road and the 3rd Battalion on the left (South). Limited objective was assigned (From "Point "F" to "Point "B" and to the Northwest.) Machine gun preparation was fired by "H" and "M" Companies for half hour preceeding attack.

At 0930 Company "I" arrived at "Point C".
At 1025 Company "E" advanced toward "Point B" from its location at "Point E".

At the same time Company "L" jumped off from "Point C" and advanced toward their objective along the ridge running South. At the same time Company "G" commenced a northern encirclement from "Point E" to attack OP Hill from the North.

All companies had forward observers from artillery and fire of opportunity was brought down on all enemy resistance. Attacks were supported by heavy 60mm and 81mm Mortar Fire, and the 2nd Battalion had 4.2 Mortar forward

Newsweek

NOVEMBER 27, 194_

Slow, Muddy, and Nasty
Battle of the Leyte Spider Holes
One of War's Hardest, Bloodiest

The incredibly tedious and bloody task of rooting out the Leyte Japs is described graphically in this dispatch from Robert Shaplen, Newsweek war correspondent.

The command post was knee-deep in mud on the side of the hill and when we climbed up from the road it was nip and tuck whether we would make it or slide back into the quagmire below. It was pouring and although it was 10 o'clock in the morning the sky was dark. Behind us was the Philippine Sea off the east coast of Leyte, and in front were the rolling ridges which for eleven muddy days had already provided the stiffest battleground in the history of the Southwest Pacific. This was where fresh, crack Jap troops, landed at Ormoc 15 miles to the south, were being deployed by General Yamashita along a jagged mountain and valley line. This was the second phase of the Leyte battle—a first-rate Jap delaying action and maybe something more.

Charlie The Sniper: Col. William Verbeck, commanding officer of the 21st Regiment of the 24th Division, sat at the phones talking to his forward observers. "We'll attack at 10:30," the colonel said. "Use your flame throwers and we'll give you fifteen minutes of 81 mortar before them. How's that?"

The other end of the wire expressed approval and the colonel rang off. "Sit here and listen to the concert," the colonel invited.

It began frighteningly and prematurely with a ten-minute burst from Jap 75-millimeter artillery, crashing 200 yards to our left. Then our mortars began whoomphing overhead. Between roars, the flat, snapping note of a Jap sniper's rifle sounded just above us.

"That's Charlie," said Colonel Verbeck. "He always gets excited when the show starts."

Excited or not, Charlie had been up there in the cogon grass, which is as high as New Guinea's kunai, for several days and had already killed about fifteen Americans, including Frank Prist, Acme photographer (see page 36). Charlie was good and he had one of the world's best hiding places.

We heard the concert put and then moved up along the road in the jeep of Maj. Gen. F. C. Sibert, commander of the Tenth Corps. Brig. Gen. Kenneth Cramer, assistant commander of the 24th, rode in back with General Sibert while your correspondent crouched in front, flanked by two MP's with guns cocked. Slowly we eased along the side of the hill and then inched up the ridge, which an unknown private had aptly dubbed Breakneck in the middle of the week-long fight to take it. The ridge was saucer-shaped and there were few trees on it. It was pocked by ravines and round the gullies the grass was 6 feet high. The smell of Jap dead floated sickly over it.

Two Ridges: Near the summit, we got out and started crawling. From the top we watched the progress of the battle for the next ridge, still unnamed, 50 yards away. The mortar fire was landing in green, black bursts on the forward slope, and behind it was the incessant chatter of machine-gun fire, ours and the Japs'. Two of our companies were seeking to flank the hill from the sides but it was slow going.

A private shouted up to us from a pit. "Better duck," he said. "They've been sniping over here and we had some Jap artillery a few minutes ago."

Burning Out Spiders: There was nothing sensational about this fight in the Ormoc corridor. It was just slow, muddy, and nasty. Probably nowhere else have Japs been dug in so well. Their favorite position was in a spider hole. Spider holes are one-man foxholes. They are usually 2 feet wide at the top and wider at the bottom and run from 4 to 6 feet in depth. The Japs like to place machine guns in them or just lie and wait with rifles and fistfuls of grenades. In addition to the spider holes, the Nips had the usual number of coconut-log bunkers and pillboxes as well as the natural ally of the cogon grass. They made a point of burrowing into both sides of every slope, and downhill the reverse sides of the ridges were as difficult to capture as the ascending slopes.

The 24th Division had to advance by inches, using grenades, flame throwers, and rifles. Tanks were employed along the route where feasible but the rainy season in the Philippines is poor tank weather. Most effective were light and medium American artillery and the constant blanket of mortar fire over the hill. Phosphorus fire, spewed by mortar over wide areas with the aid of the wind, burned out large areas of Jap resistance.

Food and Blood: The supply problem was critical throughout. Ammunition and food bogged down on washed-out roads and bulldozers had to pull dozens of trucks through. The strategy employed by the 24th, in which one regiment worked down the road and two regiments flanked it on both sides, leapfrogging from ridge to ridge, created a need for food drops from planes. But when the planes came back shot full of holes, native carriers and carabaos had to be used exclusively.

The casualties in the division, which has been in line 27 consecutive days, and was responsible for killing some 5,500 Japs, ran as high as 50 per cent among combat troops. Much of this was due to snipers.

Advances were limited to 400 or 500 yards a day along the road. The Nips almost always counterattacked late in the afternoon, and if the Americans over-extended their lines they lost the ground they had gained. So they made a point of attacking in the morning, consolidating and waiting for the Japs to recoil.

observers and used this fire to great advantage.

In a grenade, rifle and flame thrower action the remaining pocket in the gulch just East of "Points C and E" was eliminated.

At 1150 Company "L" reported heavy rifle and mortar fire slowing its advance.

At 1305 Company "L" was still progressing on the top of the ridge in the center of its zone of action.

At 1335 Company "G" reported having taken its objective but due to heavy enemy fire of all weapons was organizing the Eastern slopes of the ridge 300 yards North of "Point B".

At 1815 Company "G" received counter-attacks which were repulsed. At dark the forward line was as follows: Company "F" at "Point F", Company "L" at "Point G", Company "I" at "Point C", Company "E" in the vicinity of high ground just Northwest of "Point B", and Company "G" on East slope of ridge 300 yards North of "Point B". A platoon of heavy machine guns was attached to each rifle company to tie in their perimeters for the night. Company "K" was in reserve near "Point A". 400 Japanese bodies were counted during this day's action.

An agressive mission was assigned to the Regiment for the next day. The front of the Regiment was reduced by the assignment of Hill 1525 to the 19th Infantry.

10 November 1944: The night and morning of 10 November 1944, the weather was heavy rain, and the ground was intensely muddy. During the night the enemy cut wire lines to the forward battalions. Message from X Corps, 10 November 1944 relayed through Headquarters 24th Division stated: "Early arrival of reinforcements expected."

Casualties of the Regiment at this time had reached, 72 Killed in Action, 232 Wounded, 7 Missing. Officer casualties were especially high.

Division Field Order No. 8, dated, 2310, 9 November is quoted in part:

"2. 24th Division will attack with four (4) battalions in assault enveloping hostile left (West) flank, secure objective and protect the Corps West Flank.
    Time of attack: 0700.

"3. a. 21st Infantry reinforced:
    Will attack with two (2) battalions in assault, seize and hold its portion of the Division objective prepared to continue the attack.

    b. 19th Infantry (-2 Battalions):
    Will attack with one battalion from present positions in the vicinity of Hill 1525 seize and hold its portion of the Division objective. (Note: This Battalion was not actually on Hill 1525.)

    c. 34th Infantry reinforced (-1 Battalion):
    (1) Will have 1st Battalion under Division control assemble CAPOOCAN BEACH not later than 0500, 10 November 1944. Move over water by LVT, land (2 miles West of PINAMOPOAN) attack, capture and hold its portion of Division objective.

X. Success of the LEYTE campaign depends upon quickly and completely destroying hostile forces now to our front."

The following is extracted from Headquarters X Corps, Weekly Report No. 3, dated 11 November 1944:

"10 November 1944, the 24th Infantry Division failed to move forward, and enemy resistance continued strong. However a pocket of resistance on North Slope of BREAKNECK RIDGE was eliminated."

The following is extracted from Headquarters 24th Division Periodic Report No. 22, 1800, 10 November 1944:

"All efforts to move down or around the reverse slopes of high ground just East of the road (06.6-66.6) were met by heavy small arms and automatic weapons fire. Intermittant artillery fire received by forward elements of the 21st Infantry at close of period. Forward artillery observers believe that they have located the enemy artillery positions and counter battery fire is being effected. Enemy bodies counted in day's action by 21st Infantry - 78".

"It is estimated that the 21st Infantry, was now opposed to at least 2 Battalions of the Japanese 57th Infantry Regiment, and at least 1 Battalion of the 49th Infantry Regiment. Identifications also were found confirming presence of the 1st Infantry Regiment to our front. These are three Infantry Regiments of the First Division, recently arrived from Manchuria. Enemy troops are well trained, well equipped and fed and appear to be first class fighting soldiers."

At 0930, the 1st Battalion moved forward in column of companies, Company "A" leading, and passed through Company "K" and moved south. Company "K" was at this time at "Point E".

At 0955 Company "G" took OP Hill. At the same time Company "I" moved to bridge and guarded it.

1st Platoon, Company "A", 3rd Engineers began reconstruction of the bridge to permit the passage of tanks. This bridge building job, carried out under fire, was an accomplishment of the 1st Platoon, Company "A", 3rd Engineers. The enemy had destroyed the bridge and Captain Latane, "A" Company commander, had measured the distance to be spanned. He took the figures back and timbers were cut to the exact size. The structure virtually prefabricated was trucked as near the gulch as possible and the bridge was assembled under fire.

At 1120, Company "L" seized the high ground 300 yards South of its previous day's position and held commanding ground ("Point H"). At 1010 the enemy pocket of resistance between "G" and "L" Companies was cleared out and the entire ridge was thus secured.

The 1st Battalion was directed to attack the ridge 200 yards to its front (West) by maneuvering in the draws on either side of the enemy held spur. This attack failed to materialize. At the close of the day found the 1st Battalion on its morning positions. The 1st Battaion Commander was relieved and Major Little, Executive Officer, 3rd Battalion was placed in command.

Company "G" was relieved by Company "A" and Company "G" withdrew to the perimeter held by Company "K".

At 1535 Company "L" received strong artillery fire.

The Battalion of the 34th Infantry on the right and the 19th Infantry on the left were in rear of the extension of the flanks of the 21st Infantry and were believed to be moving south to come abreast of the 21st Infantry. Supplying rations and ammunition to the scattered units still presented the greatest threat to the success of the operation. At no time was more than a unit of fire present in the Regiment.

11 November 1944: During the night 10-11 November 1944 the enemy cut telephone lines from Regiment to all Battalions. Headquarters X Corps Weekly Report No. 3, is quoted in part as follows:

"11 November 1944, the 21st Infantry penetrated the enemy strongpoint on the South slope of BREAKNECK RIDGE. This was the second of two pockets which had offered resistance for three days. Breakthrough was accomplished with the assistance of eleven tanks. Fifteen out of twenty known heavy machine gun positions were eliminated. The pocket of resistance has not been cleared but has been considerably weakened."

For the period 115 enemy bodies were counted.

At 0805 a message received that the 1st Battalion, 34th Infantry on our right was moving towards their objective south and west of LIMON. Heavy intermittent rains throughout the day with very slippery mud underfoot. Artillery preparation was to be fired for one hour prior to 0900 on enemy ridges and pockets along BREAKNECK RIDGE. Company "C" 85th Chemical Battalion maintained harrassing fire on reverse slopes South of "Points, F, H, G" and OP Hill at the rate of approximately two rounds every five minutes all night. From 0645 to 0745 concentration of 750 rounds were to be fired and from 0830-0900 a concentration of White Phosphorous was to be fired. Forward observers with each rifle company for Artillery, 4.2 Mortars and 81mm Mortars were to bring down fire of opportunity on all enemy points of resistance. At 0900 the 1st and 2nd Battalions jumped off abreast 1st Battalion on the right (North of OP Hill). The 2nd Battalion in column of companies attacked to the South and West. Company "E" moved through Company "F" and attacked South. Company "G" attacked Northwest along the ridge in the direction of OP Hill to connect with the 1st Battalion.

Company "I" was held at "Point C" with one platoon guarding the bridge. The attack of the 2nd Battalion towards the South met strong enemy resistance almost immediately from the South and from wooded ridges to the East of CORKSCREW. At 0955, Company "G" in 2nd Battalion reserve was moved up to CORKSCREW. Company "L" still attached to the 2nd Battalion attacked the resistance to the East and met heavy resistance from woods 150 yards to the East. Company "F" along Hot Spot Knob, in the meanwhile had passed through Company "E", observed 150 Japanese digging in on the ridge to their east. They brought down heavy mortar and machine gun fire on this position, and then attacked and occupied the ridge with one platoon. At first this position was believed to constitute the heavy enemy resistance from the east, but "E", "G" and "L" Companies still found their southward operations were flanked by heavy fire from the East. The terrain was such that a 200 yard advance represented a 500 yard movement on the terrain.

LEGION OF MERIT

Master Sergeant CHARLES H. BANKS, R651287, Infantry, United States Army. For exceptionally meritorious conduct in the performance of outstanding services in the Hawaiian Islands and the Southwest Pacific Area from December 1941 to June 1945. As personnel Sergeant Major and subsequently Regimental Sergeant Major, 21st Infantry, Sergeant Banks did much to bring the Regiment to strength, and selected, assigned and trained an entirely new administrative staff in preparation for combat operations. Following six months of almost continuous combat, he thoroughly processed accumulated administrative personnel matters in addition to handling current matters passing through headquarters. Later during the Mindanao operation, by frequent visits to the front lines he familiarized himself with job requirements and personnel needs in all units. He processed individually each of 1300 replacements in order to assure their proper assignment. By skillful and expeditious handling of the administration of his headquarters, especially at times when its strength was critically low Sergeant Banks played a most important role in the outstanding performance of the 21st Infantry in Combat.

BRONZE STAR

Chaplain (Capt.) KARL A. UFER, O-460820, Corps of Chaplains, United States Army. For heroic achievement in connection with military operations against the enemy at Breakneck Ridge, Leyte Island, Philippine Islands, from 5 November to 20 November 1944. Chaplain Ufer as Regimental Chaplain, 21st Infantry, 24th Infantry Division brought spiritual morale to the battlefield. During this period the regiment was engaged in offensive operations against a numerically superior enemy and in spite of heavy casualties continued forward movement. Chaplain Ufer, feeling that spiritual encouragement could best be imparted to the Combat Infantryman at the point where the fighting was the fiercest and where danger was greatest, moved to these points along the front of the 21st Infantry and gave spiritual cheer and encouragement to the men. He was under almost constant threat of death or injury from enemy fire. Daily he went to the forefront to recover and identify bodies on the battlefield. Had it not been for the activities of Chaplain Ufer under fire, numbers of our dead would still be listed as missing in action. After the regiment was relieved from combat and moved to a reserve area on 16 November 1944, Chaplain Ufer returned to the battlefield where troops of the 32nd Division were still heavily engaged and continued the finding and identifying of our dead. On one day during this period of 16-20 November 1944, the enemy infiltrated behind the point where he was working and cut off his route of withdrawal. He continued with his work until the way was reopened. Chaplain Ufer's devotion to duty was an inspiration to every member of the 21st Infantry Regiment and reflects great credit upon himself and the military service.

Rev. Karl A. Ufer
Chaplain of the 21st Infantry

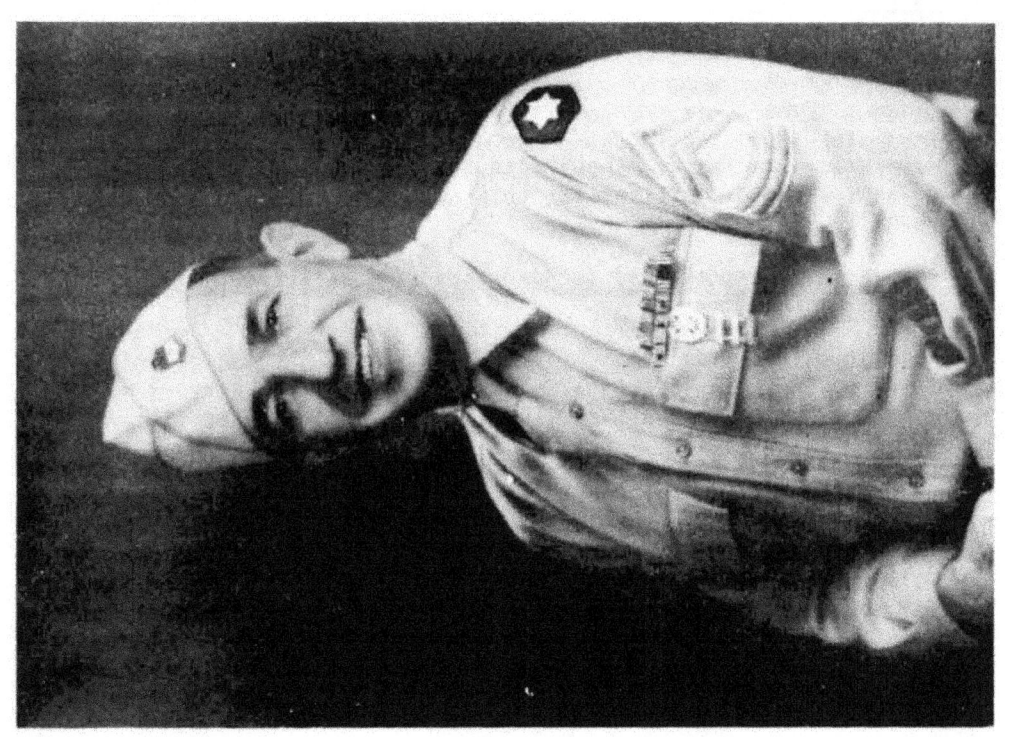

Master Sergeant Charles Banks
Regimental Sgt. Major 21st Infantry

The 1st Battalion's advance met little resistance initially. At 1320 the Engineers reported the bridge completed. The tanks would be unable to advance to the top of the BREAKNECK without support of riflemen to the front, rear and with the column due to suicide attacks by enemy soldiers with magnetic mines and grenades. The approach to the bridge to the OP Hill was known to be heavily mined. A squad of Engineer Mine Detector personnel, twelve enlisted men from the Regimental Intelligence and Reconnaissance Platoon, and a platoon from Company "I" were employed as rifle cover for the tanks in their advance up and over to the South slopes of BREAKNECK.

Captain Van Winkle, Commanding Officer of Company "A", 44th Tank Battalion led his tanks on foot and personally directed their operations under heavy fire. He was twice wounded but returned only after the operation was completed. On the section of the road running South for 300 yards from the OP Hill, the tanks, although road bound due to the nature of the terrain, engaged and destroyed numbers of pillboxes, and automatic weapons, and cleared the way for the advance of the 1st Battalion. The tanks withdrew before nightfall with the loss of one tank. The 1st Battalion gained its objective (ridge at "Point J".)

At 1815, a report was received that the 2nd Battalion, 19th Infantry was slowly moving South to a position Northeast of LIMON.

All positions were consolidated and 350 rounds of White Phosphorous were used with effect on enemy positions facing the 1st and 2nd Battalions. The wind was blowing generally south and enemy positions in spider holes were cleaned out thereby. Fields of fire were also cleared in the high cogon grass bordering our perimeters by this fire. During the days action the 1st Battalion fired 1,500 rounds of 81mm Mortar.

The following is extracted from Headquarters X Corps Weekly Report No. 4 dated 18 November 1944:

"The 12th of November 1944, the enemy resisted our advances South down the reverse slope of BREAKNECK RIDGE. However, progress was made by our forces until after 1300, when the enemy strength began to build up. By 1600, the enemy firepower had reached such a degree of intensity that our forward elements were forced to consolidate the ridge. During the night our units were harassed by infiltration into our perimeters and some artillery fire."

The G-2 Periodic Report No. 24, Headquarters 24th Infantry Division, the following is quoted:

"At the end of this period (1800, 12 November 1944) the 21st Infantry forced to consolidate their positions on BREAKNECK RIDGE by heavy enemy fire from an estimated two battalions with all arms including artillery.

During the day of 12 November 1944, the Regiment counted 97 Japanese bodies killed during the day. At 0715, 12 November, the Anti-tank Company was dispatched to the position of Company "G" to relieve them. The strength of the companies at this time was low. The 1st Battalion commanded by Major Little averaged one officer and one hundred enlisted men per company. Some returned sick, wounded, and about 50 replacements were received at this time and were split among the rifle companies. All rear echelon personnel who could be spared from their duties were sent as replacements to the rifle companies. Native carriers, in limited numbers were obtained to carry ammunition and rations to the front line companies. One hot meal per day could now be fed to combat elements. Ammunition reserves were built up to about $1\frac{1}{2}$ units of fire.

SILVER STAR

Colonel WILLIAM J. VERBECK, Infantry, United States Army. For gallantry in action near Pinamopoan, Leyte, Philippine Islands, on 11 November 1944. The regiment of infantry which Colonel Verbeck was commanding had been held up for five days by a determined Japanese force of infantry and artillery. The enemy was strongly entrenched in the gulches and on the reverse slopes of a commanding ridge about two thousand yards southwest of Pinamopoan. They were fresh first-line troops, equipped with a high percentage of automatic weapons. At this critical time Colonel Verbeck organized a striking force consisting of one platoon of medium tanks protected by the regimental intelligence and reconnaissance platoon and one engineer mine - detector squad, and personally led it on foot to the crest of the ridge, from which point the infantry and tanks were, for the first time, able to advance and hold ground. The turning point had been reached. From then on our troops were able to move steadily forward. Colonel Verbeck's example of bravery and energy had inspired his troops with the drive needed to overcome an aggressive well-trained enemy force and is in keeping with the highest of military traditions.

SILVER STAR (Posthumous)

First Lieutenant DALE E. JOHNSON, Infantry, United States Army. For gallantry in action in the vicinity of Pinamopoan, Leyte, Philippine Islands, on 11 November 1944. Lieutenant Johnson accompanied a group of his men during a tank action, the mission of his party being to protect the tanks in their advance from suicidal attempts of the enemy to lay mines under the tracks of the vehicles. During the tank action, three wounded men, left behind from the previous day's fighting, were discovered on high ground that was swept by enemy fire. Lieutenant Johnson unhesitatingly crawled to the high ground under enemy fire and, with the help of three enlisted men, evacuated these casualties to safety. He supervised the evacuation of the wounded soldiers with a calm steadiness. Later in the same action, with a small party, he occupied a ridge under heavy enemy fire and protected both flanks of the tank column with fire from this commanding terrain feature. Lieutenant Johnson was killed in a later action against the enemy. Lieutenant Johnson's courage and total disregard for his own personal safety were a source of inspiration to all who witnessed his actions, and reflect great credit upon himself and the military service.

BRONZE STAR

Captain (then First Lieutenant) SOTHORON K. ABLE, Infantry, United States Army. For heroic achievement in connection with military operations against the enemy near Pinamopoan, Leyte, Philippine Islands, on November 11, 1944. Captain Able with the remnants of his platoon of Infantry was directed to furnish rifle protection to a platoon of medium tanks. Leading the column on foot under enemy fire Captain Able escorted the tanks to the crest of an enemy held ridge 2000 yards southwest of Pinamopoan. From this point the tanks and Infantry were able to advance and hold ground. Captain Able then assisted in the removal, under fire, of our wounded who had been lying near the crest for two days. His energy and courage are a credit to himself and the military service.

View of Pinamopoan - Breakneck Ridge
Looking North to South Towards
Limon From Carigara Bay, Leyte.
11 November 1944

Lieutenant Pablo V. Bacciera, Philippine Guerrila leader reports for orders to Colonel William J. Verbeck on Leyte, Philippine Islands.

The Tribune

Year XX — Manila, Philippines, Sunday, November 12, 1944 — **Number 192**

This Issue 4 Pages | Price 20 Centavos Pay No More

Japanese Surround Mainstay Of U.S. 24th Division in Leyte

Enemy Dislodged From Positions In Carigara Sector

Nippon Forces Advancing Towards Site Of Divisional Headquarters—Supply, Communication Lines of Doomed Unit Cut

Powerful Japanese units operating in the Carigara sector have succeeded in surrounding the mainstay of the U.S. 24th Division on Tuesday, November 7, according to the latest reports reaching Manila.

Subjecting the enemy troops to a heavy concentration of artillery fire and severe attacks by land troops, the Japanese forces dislodged the enemy from his positions, and are steadily tightening their encirclement ring.

Advancing Nippon units are sweeping on to the site of the enemy 24th Divisional headquarters while other units have completely severed the flow of troops and supplies as well as communications to the enemy headquarters.

Overcoming difficult terrain, the Nippon ground units are continuing their heavy onslaught, bringing about total annihilation to the doomed enemy outfit, reports added.

Reports from other sectors were equally reassuring. Japanese garrison in the Dagami sector are still maintaining their uphill fighting against the enemy while those consolidating a stronghold at Catmon hill north of Dulag are blocking every enemy attempt to break through.

The grand-scale offensive now looming in all sectors will spell doom to the U.S. invasion forces, reports revealed.

Tacloban Airfield Raided

In uninterrupted air action over the Leyte invasion front the Japanese Army Wild Eagles at daybreak on Friday struck at the Tacloban airfield. Heavy smoke was seen rising from three flaming points, indicating the destructive power of the Nippon aerial bombardment, reports from the front lines revealed.

Meanwhile other reports brought in the news of severe dogfighting over the Ormoc area on the same day when a total of 16 enemy aircraft were either shot down or damaged out of a fighter-bomber formation which appeared over the region. Japanese airmen definitely shot down 12 P-38's and probably brought down two more besides damaging two others, the reports from the sector said.

U.S. Reports From Leyte Not So Rosy Now

TOKYO, Nov. 10 (Domei).—The hitherto fantastically optimistic American war reports from Leyte took a different turn today with predictions that the Philippine campaign may be long and hard, according to reports received here.

Typical was the dispatch sent today by Murlin Spencer, Associated Press reporter attached to General MacArthur's headquarters, stating that General MacArthur disclosed that a large group of veteran Japanese troops had run through the gauntlet of harassing fire from American planes and motor torpedo boats and had joined in the sanguinary battle for Leyte. Spencer said General MacArthur's announcement indicates that the "battle for the Philippines may be long and hard."

The attack plan was for the 3rd Battalion under Lt.Colonel Ramee with the Tank Company attached to continue the attack East astride the road on the top of BREAKNECK RIDGE. All Regimental flame throwers were supplied to the 3rd Battalion. After the tanks had crossed the crest the 1st Battalion was to attack on the right, and envelop the enemy's left (West) flank. 2nd Battalion in reserved between "Points F and H".

At 1045, the 3rd Battalion jumped off. At the same time the Anti-Tank Company reported securing the ridge in front of Company "G" last night position.

At 1115, the tanks were beyond the cut on the ridge and reported receiving very little hostile fire.

At 1125 Company "C" took its objective (Hill at "Point K").

At 1135, Companies "L" & "F" took their objectives at "Points M and N", respectively and were concentrating their fire on the draw between their positions.

At 1220, Companies "F" and "K" had made contact at Point "O", and the whole of BREAKNECK RIDGE had been taken. 3rd Battalion reported reaching its days objective.

At 1415, the Intelligence and Reconnaissance Platoon of Regimental Headquarters was sent out to mop up snipers overlooking the bridge. Reported successful mission. Sniper fire in our rear elements ceased for the first time after this action.

At 1545, all front line units reported that enemy fire to their front and flanks was increasing and that the enemy was being reinforced. No further advances were made. Consolidated perimeters were set up for the night. There was little enemy activity and no counter-attacks were made during the night.

2,200 rounds of 81mm Mortar were expended during the day.

13 November 1944: As will be discerned by glancing at the map BREAKNECK RIDGE is not one ridgeline but in reality is a series of six ridges none of which are continuous but are formed by a series of knobs. The low ground is thick with cogon grass to a height of four feet. The pockets between the hills are rugged and thickly wooded. The valleys are deep, precipitous. Although all commanders constantly endeavored to prevent the attack from breaking up into a series of uncoordinated combats, the terrain did not permit exact timing or coordination. Jump off times were often postponed due to the difficulties of supply of ammunition.

Headquarters X Corps Weekly Report No. 4, had the following report concerning the action of the 21st Infantry, for 13 November 1944:

"During the day the 21st Infantry advanced South from BREAKNECK RIDGE, and at 1500 were 400-600 yards South of the crest of the ridge. At that time the right flank (West) of the road was not in contact, while the left flank (East) of the road was encountering some resistance. At this time an enemy attack developed from the crest with approximate strength of one company but the attack was repulsed and the Japanese withdrew."

G-2 Periodic Report No. 25, Headquarters 24th Infantry Division, is quoted as follows:

"Enemy identifications at BREAKNECK RIDGE - 57th Infantry, Headquarters

SILVER STAR

First Lieutenant PHILIP S. IRONS, III, Infantry, United States Army. For gallantry in action at Pinamopoan Ridge, Leyte, Philippine Islands, on 13 November 1944. An infantry company was given the mission of attacking and occupying two hills, two hundred yards to the left of a mountain road. This ground controlled the road for four hundred yards. The company succeeded in occupying the extreme left hill which secured the left flank, but the platoon on the right flank was forced to withdraw. During this operation the company commander was seriously wounded. At approximately 1400, Lieutenant Irons, belonging to another organization, was sent forward to assume command of the company with the mission of seizing the second hill and holding it all at costs. The enemy was well entrenched and was in possession of commanding ground with good observation. Lieutenant Irons reorganized a greatly depleted unit of very tired men and seized the second hill after much hard fighting. Later in the evening, after the second hill was seized, he organized the defense of the hill with hardly sufficient personnel for adequate security. During the night his company was fiercely attacked by the enemy with grenades and bayonets. This enemy attack was repulsed. The number of dead during this operation was two hundred. Lieutenant Iron's leadership and courage were a source of inspiration to all members of his company, and reflects great credit upon himself and the military service.

BRONZE STAR

Technician Fifth Grade FLOYD K. GULBRANSON, Medical Department, United States Army. For heroic achievement in connection with military operations against the enemy at Breakneck Ridge, Leyte, Philippine Islands, from 12 November to 18 November 1944. As medical aid man for an engineer working party, Technician Gulbranson was the only medical man in the vicinity. He rendered quick and efficient aid to wounded infantrymen as well as his own unit. He was constantly under fire from enemy snipers, but carried out his work calmly and effectively. Technician Gulbranson's conduct under fire reflects greatest credit upon himself and the military service.

SILVER STAR

Private First Class HARVEY H. PERRY, Medical Department, United States Army. For gallantry in action at Breakneck Ridge, Leyte, Philippine Islands, on 16 November 1944. On this day Private Perry, a medical aid man for an engineering working party found it necessary to render first aid to men from other organizations who were without medical assistance. He rendered the required aid quickly and efficiently without regard for his personal safety. Later a man from his own unit was hit and the entire party pinned down by enemy machine gun fire. Private Perry went fearlessly to his aid. In doing so his first aid pouches were ripped from his back by machine gun fire. he continued his errand of mercy, however, and evacuated the wounded man safely. On this as well as on numerous other occasions, Private Perry's conduct was a heroic example for the other men of his organization and the armed forces of his country.

SILVER STAR

Staff Sergeant (then Private First Class) JOHN W. McCLELLAND, Infantry, United States Army. For gallantry in action at Leyte, Philippine Islands, on 12 November 1944. Sergeant McClelland was acting assistant squad leader of an infantry rifle company. After his platoon had attacked a strongly defended Japanese perimeter and succeeded in penetrating it, he was ordered to guard the rear of his platoon. In this capacity, he personally accounted for six Japanese trying to infiltrate the position and isolate the platoon. Sergeant McClelland's fire, in the face of superior enemy numbers, was entirely responsible for keeping his platoon from being surrounded and cut off. Sergeant McClelland's courageous action reflects great credit upon himself and the military service.

BRONZE STAR

Private First Class GEORGE H. DIEHL, Infantry, United States Army. For heroic achievement in connection with military operations against the enemy at Hill 1525, Leyte, Philippine Islands, on 10 November 1944. Private Diehl was an acting squad leader in an infantry rifle company which was engaged in combat with the enemy. Exposing himself to enemy fire he worked his way to three wounded men and successively assisted each of them in reaching safety. Private Diehl's courage and devotion to his fellow soldiers reflect great credit upon himself and the military service.

BRONZE STAR

Staff Sergeant WILLIAM F. FRANCHER, Infantry, United States Army. For heroic achievement in connection with military operations against the enemy at Leyte, Philippine Islands, on 12 November 1944. Sergeant Francher was an acting platoon sergeant of an infantry rifle company. Sergeant Francher was wounded by enemy artillery shrapnel but remained at his post directing mortar fire until the company was relieved. He later had his wounds dressed but refused to be evacuated to a hospital. Sergeant Francher's actions were an inspiration to his fellow soldiers and reflect credit upon himself and the military service.

BRONZE STAR

Staff Sergeant J. D. HAMRICK, Infantry, United States Army. For heroic achievement in connection with military operations against the enemy at Leyte, Philippine Islands, on 12 November 1944. Sergeant Hamrick, a squad leader in an infantry rifle company, during the heaviest barrage of artillery and mortar fire, left the comparative safety of his foxhole to rescue one of his wounded men at the risk of his own life. Sergeant Hamrick's courageous action set an excellent example for his men and reflects great credit upon himself and the military service.

SILVER STAR

Private First Class JACK FURMAN, Infantry, United States Army. For gallantry in action at Breakneck Ridge, Leyte, Philippine Islands, on 13 November 1944. Private Furman was twice wounded in action against the enemy but insisted on staying with his unit. Later the same day, while the company was halted at the battalion command post on its way back to a rest area, the battalion command post received a surprise attack by a strong Japanese force. Private Furman rushed at once to the outer perimeter where his fire was instrumental in silencing a Japanese machine gun. His resourceful actions were an inspiration to his unit throughout the campaign.

SILVER STAR

First Lieutenant CLAUDE H. HALL, Infantry, United States Army. For gallantry in action at Leyte, Philippine Islands, on 12 November 1944. On this day, Lieutenant Hall, platoon leader, while severely wounded, and at further risk of his life, exposed himself to enemy fire to direct artillery fire upon advancing Japanese troops and an active enemy field piece. Lieutenant Hall's aggressiveness and leadership under fire served as a continuous example and inspiration to the whole company and reflects great credit upon himself and the military service.

NEW YORK HERALD TRIBUNE

NOVEMBER 15, 1944

Reporter at Leyte After Europe Finds It's Different Kind of War

Notes Scarcity of Japanese Artillery and Land Mines, Little Noise of Battle—But Snipers' Bullets Kill Man Just as Dead as Nazis' Railroad Rifles

By Homer Bigart

By Wireless to the Herald Tribune. Copyright, 1944, New York Herald Tribune Inc.

WITH THE 24TH DIVISION, Northern Leyte, Nov. 14.—The Ormoc road skirts the blue crescent of Carigara Bay and, quitting the last forlorn settlement of nipa huts, curves abruptly southward through a palm and bamboo wilderness matted with six-foot kogan grass. Ascending steeply, it traverses the first of five ridges damming the narrow defile through the interior mountains.

Across this pass, through which General Douglas MacArthur's men must move to seize Ormoc and complete the liberation of Leyte, General Tomoyuki Yamashita, the conqueror of Singapore, has flung the 1st Imperial Division.

In the opinion of Colonel William J. Verveck, of Manlius, N. Y., the 1st Division is the best in the Japanese Army. Verveck should know. As assistant military attaché in Tokyo he watched the 1st parade on Emperor Day. And for the last week his troops have carried the ball in the American attack, wresting Breakneck Ridge from the 1st Imperials in the heaviest fighting of the Leyte campaign.

Verveck's command post was a circle of foxholes in a trampled clearing. Breakneck Ridge raised its green wall nearly a mile southward. The crest is firmly held, yet Japanese snipers, crawling through the grass on the open left flank, sometimes have infiltrated far inside the defense perimeter. Two days ago a sniper picked off a photographer on the road for the fourth press fatality in the Philippine campaign.

[It was revealed at General MacArthur's headquarters on Leyte that Frank Prist, thirty-year-old Acme News photographer, had been killed by enemy fire in the Ormoc sector on Nov. 13.]

The dry bark of a sniper's rifle occasionally could be heard as Colonel Verveck told us something of the 1st Division and the tactics it pursues.

"They are just as tough and nasty as I figured they would be," said Verveck. "Back in Tokyo the Imperial Guard had a comparable reputation—they were easily the best in the Russo-Japanese War—but now they are merely snow troops assigned to the Emperor's palace. Every one conceded that the 1st Division was the best field unit."

The 1st Imperials threw at least four banzai charges against Breakneck Ridge, driving off two American companies with heavy casualties on Nov. 6, and it was not until yesterday that the crest was cleared of the Japanese.

The banzai charges follow a familiar pattern. They are usually preceded by ten or fifteen minutes of sharp motaring. Then sometimes the Japanese will emerge from cover in rank formation, like the British at Bunker Hill, running abreast with fixed bayonets.

Tactics Changed

But the 1st Imperials are too smart for that. At Breakneck they crawled to within ten or twenty feet of the American fox holes before charging. Invariably they were led by a junior officer, with saber in one hand and a nambu pistol in the other.

Each Japanese carries a sackful of grenades attached to his belt and a bolt-operated 25-calibre rifle which, with the bayonet, measures five feet. The rifle is older than our Springfield and much less accurate.

At night, in the quiet before a banzai rush, the doughboys can hear tapping sounds from the Japanese lines. That is the Japanese knocking grenades against stones to release the detonators. Sometimes the Americans can hear the Japanese officer's "blood for the Emperor" harangue that generally precedes an assault.

"Strictly speaking, there is no such thing as a banzai charge," said Verveck. "Some Japs are always yelling banzai even on defense. Banzai can mean a lot of things. They scream it at baseball games. At banquets it is a toast—'May you live a thousand years.' But in battle it always means, 'May the Emperor live a thousand years.'"

Use English Profanity

The Japanese invariably whoop and holler while attacking, and they do not always say banzai. They have picked up a few bits of English profanity, the favorite being "goddam Yanks."

Survivors of the receiving end of a banzai charge say that the banzai shouts are less bloodcurdling than the Rebel yell, but sufficiently disconcerting. Private First Class Vincent J. Davey, of 878 New York Avenue, Brooklyn, one of the last to quit Breakneck in the face of a Japanese attack, described the banzai shout thus: "It had kind of a weird sound, like Ladies' Day at Ebbets Field."

I have seen some dead Imperials along the road. They wore greenish woolen shirts, old woolen wrap leggings and khaki breeches.

Technical Sergeant Andrew E. Priestas, of Conneautville, Pa., who has been in the Pacific since Pearl Harbor, said they were the best-dressed Japanese he had run across. "Moreover, they are well built. Those that are not tall are plenty husky. Apparently they are fed better than the scrawny runts we have been meeting. Each had a sackful of rice, dried fish, hard biscuits and tea."

This correspondent, coming from the European fronts, has been impressed by the weakness of the Japanese artillery and the failure of the enemy to employ mines with anything like the diabolical thoroughness of Field Marshal Albert Kesselring's army in Italy.

The 1st Imperials have perhaps four 75s on the Ormoc Road. Their fire has been woefully ineffective, except against an easy point-blank target such as the Americans presented in the first seizure of Breakneck and before they were dug in. The Japanese are said to have heavier guns at Ormoc, but have not succeeded in hauling them over the road, which dwindles into a forest track several miles short of Breakneck. Moreover, both Ormoc and the entire length of the Japanese-held Ormoc Road are under the harassing fire of American Long Toms.

Few Mines Encountered

Few mines, whether anti-tank or anti-personnel, have been encountered. In eight days of action on the Ormoc Road the Americans have lost only one tank. That happened Sunday, when a Japanese jumped out of a ditch and placed a magnetic mine on the tracks of a tank which was blasting enemy machine-gun positions on the reverse slope of Breakneck.

Here you can drive right up to the front line in broad daylight without drawing a storm of artillery or getting blown sky high by Teller mines. And that is precisely why more correspondents have been killed here than in any comparable period in the European theater.

The newsomer gets a false sense of security. Hearing none of the usual din of battle, he comes jeeping along, admiring the scenery, when — ping — a sniper's bullet shatters his day dreams. You have only to make one excursion to the front to realize that this is a very different kind of war, and that Japanese bullets and knee mortars can kill just as surely as Colonel General Eberhard von Mackensen's railway guns at Anzio.

The knee mortar has been the most effective weapon of the Japanese in the Ormoc drive. It is a 40-mm. job, used for close-in work at forty to 400 yards.

Of course, it is silly to generalize on the fighting quality of the Japanese as compared with the Germans. Both are masters of camouflage and infiltration. Perhaps one generalization is permissible—the German is perceptibly more civilized, and rarely tries suicide tactics. When a mission becomes hopeless, the German gives up. But the Japanese never does.

Carbines Always Carried

It is the 1st Division's custom to send nightly patrols through the American lines. These patrols attempt to reach artillery and other installations far to the rear. Even at this correspondent's billet five miles from the Japanese lines, all ranks carry carbines outside the inclosure, even when venturing only as far as the mess shack, 200 yards away.

The Japanese basic infantry weapon is a light automatic rifle. It is inferior to our own Garand, but the Imperials have enough of them, plus 30-caliber machine guns, to put up a very respectable volume of fire.

Like the Germans, the Japanese favor reverse slopes, digging spider holes some distance below the crest as protection against direct fire. They seldom use bunkers except in marshy terrain. Spider holes are round and generally less than sixteen inches across, but deep enough for standing. In front of every spider hole the Japanese cut fire lanes through the kogan grass. The lanes are cut low, so that even crawling doughboys are exposed to fire. Thick grass provides excellent cover.

NEWS ACCOUNTS

GREENSBORO, NORTH CAROLINA. November 17, 1944
GREENSBORO DAILY NEWS. AMERICANS TIGHTEN GRIP ON JAP SALIENT AT LIMON, ISOLATE 3,000 ENEMY SOLDIERS. Allied Headquarters, Leyte, Friday, Nov. 17.- (U.P.) American troops of the 24th Division and the First Cavalry Division today tightened their grip on the Japanese salient at Limon where an estimated 3,000 enemy forces holding the northernmost bastion of the Yamashita Line have been virtually cut off, General Douglas MacArthur announced. Long range artillery fire continued to rake enemy positions throughout the Ormoc Corridor, creating havoc in the Japanese rear positions as Major General Fredrick A. Irving's veteran infantrymen in the north closed their trap on the enemy forces.

A United Press dispatch described American activities around Breakneck Ridge on the road between Limon and Ormoc where the 24th had closed in from east and west, as the lull before the storm. While the assault troops crept forward, probing the Japanese "spider holes" foxholes and often engaging in bayonet fighting, elements commanded by Col. William Verbeck cautiously reconnoitered the valley, and positions leading to the next rise beyond Breakneck Ridge. Verbeck's troops have advanced about 700 yards in 24 hours during which time they counted 558 Japanese dead.

NEW YORK TIMES, Wednesday Nov. 15, 1944.
IRVING TROOPS TIGHTEN NOOSE. WITH THE 24TH DIVISION. Driving toward Ormoc, Nov. 14 (U.P.) - Major General Fred Irving's troops were today fast enveloping several thousand Japanese troops on a two mile corridor between Calibao and Breakneck Ridge after smashing an enemy counter-attack late yesterday in hand to hand fighting. General Irving launched a brilliantly planned maneuver, sending strong elements around through the hills to Calibao and cut the road to prevent reinforcements from reaching the Japanese near Breakneck Ridge. Some of the Japanese may break out of the trap but they will be in small parties.

"I'm anxious to get into Limon to see the damage we must have inflicted upon the enemy." General Irving said.

The Japanese paid dearly for their counter-attack yesterday. Our forces held their ground and as the advance progressed today, Col. William Verbeck's seasoned troops started hand-to-hand fighting with the Japanese entrenched in deep fox-holes. The holes have covers over them, and as soon as the Americans pass the Japanese open up from the rear. The going was necessarily slow. The Americans advanced about 400 yards but every inch of the ground was securely held and scores of Japanese paid with their lives.

Colonel Verbeck's troops have been fighting virtually without relief for twenty-three days. Many of the troops have been unable even to change their socks and none of the men have had their battle clothes off for three weeks. But, the morale is of the highest degree.

CHICAGO SUN. BY DOWLING.--November 13, 1944.
Before rolling south and securing Pinamapoan Pass we were held to the coastal road between Carigara and Pinamapoan with Caragara Bay on our right and the mountains to our left - in military terms, a defile -. It was the logical place for the Japs to stop our Ormoc drive and they tried it, but they didn't get there in time with enough. The 21st Regiment, now led by Colonel William J. Verbeck, veteran of the Attu Campaign, was closing in on the Japs in their bottleneck position leading into the Ormoc Valley. The outcome of the campaign for Ormoc is about to begin.

Japs as Seen By Themselves

As Seen By Us

3rd Battalion, 57th Infantry Regiment, 10th Company, 57th Infantry, 1st Battalion, 1st Field Artillery Regiment; 1st Platoon, 1st Company, 1st Engineers; 57th Regiment plus 1st Battalion. Quick firing guns, 57th Regiment Gun Company, 1st Field Hospital. Enemy killed and counted during the day by the 21st Infantry - 135."

At 1130 the 1st Battalion jumped off on the right of the Regimental Front. Company "A" passed through Company "B" at 1100 and advanced. The attack was supported by Machine Gun fire from the vicinity of OP Hill firing into the draw. The tanks were held up by heavy Anti-Tank fire at the southern exit from the draw along the road. Company "B" attacked on the right flank down into the valley between "Point K and P." It made a wide envelopment of hill "P" moving onto it from the West. At 1300 Company "G" (less one platoon) replaced Company "F". Company "G" was on the left flank of the ridge. 1 platoon Company "E" was East thereof as further flank protection. At 1305, Company "A" had taken objective "Point Q". Company "B" was moving with little opposition.

At 1410, Company "G" reported being counter-attacked from the left (East).

At 1510, Companies "E" and "C" were being counter-attacked. Company "B" was called back to help hold the position of Company "C" which was threatened. All counter-attacks were repulsed. At 1525 the tanks withdrew due to poor visibility. Rain storms prevented their proper use, and ammunition was almost exhausted.

At 1550, Company "F" and the 2nd Battalion Command Post received strong counter-attacks from the East at their position at "Point R". These attacks were repulsed.

At 1710, all units of the 2nd Battalion were receiving and repulsing counter-attacks.

At 1620 Company "L" was ordered to relieve Company "F". 1800 all positions held and consolidated. The 2nd Battalion estimated it killed 342 Japanese. The heavy rains commenced again at 1800.

14 November 1944: Extracts from the Periodic Report No. 26, Headquarters 24th Infantry Division, dated 1800, 14 November 1944.

"Japanese resistance in the area of BREAKNECK RIDGE is believed to be broken. With complete occupation of the ridge area to include minor high ground to the South, superior observation and fields of fire allowed the 21st Infantry to obtain the maximum results with Machine Gun, Mortar, and Artillery during the day. Particularly good results were gained from improved fields of fire for the automatic weapons. A combined Infantry team of the 19th Infantry observed from Hill 1525, locating targets for the 21st Infantry, 81mm Mortar Crews. Enemy forces in this area suffered heavy casualties for the period. At 1700 enemy resistance consisted primarily of pockets astride the PINAMOPOAN - ORMOC Road approximately 1,200 yards North of LIMON.

The 21st Infantry counted 310 Japanese dead during the day."

At 0930, units of the 19th Infantry reported from Hill 1525. At 1030 the Regimental Intelligence and Reconnaissance Platoon was dispatched to Company "B" from there to conduct a patrol to the West of LIMON.

At 1110, Company "F" was relieved and moved back to "Point A" in Regimental Reserve.

At 1120 3rd Battalion was ordered to relieve the 1st Battalion on the right of BREAKNECK RIDGE.

At 1230, 1st Battalion had attained its objective along the line "Point Q - Point P". Company "B" took "Point P" by an encirclement to the West. The advance of the 1st Battalion was supported by tanks one of which was knocked out.

15 November 1944: During the night the 2nd Battalion commanded by Lt. Colonel Seymour Madison received three desperate counter-attacks. In the last some enemy penetrated and were eliminated in a bayonet fight. Although enemy fire prohibited a count of enemy dead, the following morning large numbers of enemy were killed. Between 0900 and 1400 all Battalions employing all companies attacked and encircled remaining enemy reistances. 2nd Battalion also attacked East and eliminated enemy prockets from which its counter-attacks had been received. However, the 19th Infantry on our left had not closed the wide gap between Hill 1525 and BREAKNECK so enemy reinforcements constantly filtered in and became strong before nightfall. On the 16th of November 1944 the Regiment again attacked supported by all attached weapons and units. On the evening 16 November 1944, the 21st Infantry occupied the last remaining high ground and potential defensive positions North of LIMON.

Headquarters X Corps Weekly Report, No. 4, dated 18 November 1944 states as follows:

"15 November 1944, in the 21st Infantry sector resistance throughout the day consisted of small arms, automatic weapons, mortar and some artillery fire. Sniper fire was received throughout the day in rear of the front line elements. Many small pockets of 25-50 Japanese in rear areas were wiped out by machine gun and mortar fire. During the night the 2nd and 3rd Battalions, 21st Infantry, were attacked by 25-50 Japanese supported by 81mm Mortar Fire. Attacks were repulsed with 12 Japs killed in action in each case.

16 November 1944: The 128th Infantry passed through the 21st Infantry at 1200. During the morning the 21st Infantry had no enemy contacts but succeeded in mopping up rear areas."

On 15 November 1944, the 21st Infantry killed and wounded 245 Japanese, and on 16 November 1944 the 21st Infantry killed 47.

Battle casualties for the 21st Infantry from 5th to 16th of November-630. Sick, injured from other casuses or battle fatigue-133. Total 765.

Enemy bodies counted during the same period were 1,779.

It can be assumed that there was at least one enemy wounded for every counted dead, and also a number of dead uncounted.

At the time of the relief of the 21st Infantry by the 32nd Division, the front line was located along the line "Point "F", "L", "X", "Y".

Amicedo Farola, of Dulag, Leyte. Guerrilla Scout who Operated with the 21st Infantry. He vowed not to cut his hair until all Japanese invaders of the Philippines had been destroyed.

Major Gerald Lockhart
S-3, 21st Infantry, Wounded
Twice as C.O. Baker Company

Col. Verbeck

Lieut. Col. Eric Ramee
C.O. 3rd Battalion on
Leyte and Mindoro

1st Battalion 21st Infantry at Santa Cruz,
Mindanao, Philippine Islands, July 1, 1945.
1st Row: Lt.Doyal,Hq.Co., Lt Wisor Co B, Maj Lockhart Rgt S-3,
Lt Mullis Bn S-2, Lt.O'Donnell Surgeon, Lt Hammick MAC,
2nd Row: Chaplain Klann, Capt Counts Co C, Capt Irons Co A,
Capt Aitken Ex O, Col Verbeck, Capt Farmer S-3, Major Sloan
1st Bn Commanding Officer.

Officers of Second Battalion 21st Infantry Prior to Landing on Panaon Island
October 1944.
Front Row L to R: Lt.Col. Madison, Rgt. Ex Off, Lt. Parent F Co,
Lt Kilgo E Co, Capt Kelley G Co, Lt. Ender H Co, Major Dice Bn. C.O.,
Second Row: Lt Ivey Bn S-2, Lt Lannin Mtr Off, Lt. Lemm S-4,
Lt. Froome Com Off, Capt. Crosson Bn Ex Off, Lt Mayer S-3,
Capt. Thompson S-1, Capt. Jones Surgeon.

HEADQUARTERS 21ST INFANTRY
Office of the Regimental Commander
APO 24

15 December 1944

Subject: Enemy Tactics.

To : Asst't Chief of Staff, G-2, Sixth Army, APO #442.
  (Thru: G-2 Channels)

1. In compliance with verbal request for material for inclusion in a weekly G-2 Report, the following is submitted:

"The 21st Infantry was committed to action against strong hostile forces at PINAMOPOAN, LEYTE ISLAND, PHILIPPINE ISLANDS, on 5 November 1944. Elements in contact were 57th Infantry Regiment, 49th Infantry Regiment, and small units of the 1st Infantry Regiment all of the First Division, and a Battalion or more of the 1st Division Artillery including some 15 m guns. During the period 5 November to 16 November 1944 the Regiment was directed to "maintain the initiative at all costs". During the period the 21st Infantry suffered 630 battle casualties, and killed and counted 1,779 enemy. The twelve day period resulted in an advance of 2,000 yards of difficult terrain over a series of six ridges South of PINAMOPOAN, now called BREAKNECK RIDGE.

All who contacted the enemy were impressed with his excellence in battle. Little was noted of reckless charges, needless sacrifices, or failure to observe known tactical principles. The most outstanding enemy characteristic was his excellence in fire discipline and control of all arms. Without exception enemy fire was withheld until the moment when its delivery in great volume would give greatest effect. On 5 November 1944, the enemy on forward slopes of the first ridge allowed his positions to be by-passed by two reinforced companies of the 3rd Battalion. The enemy in approximate strength of one Battalion remained quietly in such concealment that the two companies advanced apparently without opposition on a routine relief movement and to secure the high ground. Then the enemy opened with such great effect that the two forward companies found themselves completely isolated and unable to move, receive supplies or evacuate wounded. Only by super-human efforts on the part of the remainder of the Regiment were these two companies extricated.

During the daily attacks in the following ten days there were numerous instances where enemy defensive areas often consisting of bunkers, eight to twelve machine guns, mortars and one company of riflemen would permit cautiously moving advance elements to pass their excellently concealed positions, and fire on reserve troops moving in more compact formations.

Throughout the entire period, generally speaking, enemy resistance was light in the morning and early afternoon hours.

After 1530, enemy resistance began to build up. It was extremely heavy at about 1600, and then counter-attacks from front and flanks, and between units commenced and increased in intensity until dark. Night attacks on our perimeters although frequent were not as S.O.P. as is usual with Japanese

BREAKNECK RIDGE

A Lesson in Jap Defensive Tactics

Cover Illustration—A Jap machine gun emplacement on the flank of a reverse-slope position prepares to fire at American troops advancing against Breakneck Ridge during operations on Leyte.

Enemy infiltrators would cut the telephone wire lines and then ambush the linemen who came to repair the break (page 5).

Forces. During six nights there were no enemy counter-attacks at all. By building up resistance late in the afternoon, and counter attacking in force before dark, the enemy was able to bring greatest fire, with consequent demoralizing and disorganizing effect upon our assault troops at a time when their energy and ammunition were as nearly exhausted as they would be at any time during the day. It also prevented proper consolidation of front positions before dark.

Envelopments and encirclements never forced retirement or evacuation of any enemy position. Too great emphasis had been placed on training that mere encirclement meant a successful action. The team play of the encircling force, large or small, had to be continued through the stages of occupation of the position, close combat within the position in conjunction with the frontal effort and complete mopping up.

Enemy snipers were not found in trees although many trees offered good locations. Snipers seldom if ever fired at vehicles on roads, no matter how full of personnel they appeared to be. However, snipers were constantly firing at foot troops on roads, either as single individuals or in formations. Snipers were often posted in nests of three or four. Consequently a volume of sniper fire could be delivered at once, even well behind the front lines. When firing at a single man, a group of four snipers would emit only one shot. This was apparently to conceal the location of the group. Many snipers used telescopic sights. Their fire was extremely accurate.

Enemy artillery always fired into our positions when our supporting artillery was firing in close support of our own advances. Often this caused calls from rifle units to our artillery to cease firing. Enemy mortars followed the same practice as well as enemy small arms which fired when our automatic weapons fired.

The typical shrieking, hysterical, so called Banzai Charge was noticeably not employed. Enemy counter attacks were supported by mortar fire and automatic weapons.

Our tank attacks or even movement in column to attack positions had to be guarded in front, flanks, and rear by riflemen. This was to prevent suicide attacks by Japs specifically left for that one purpose, with magnetic mines, demolitions or grenades which were inserted in the tracks.

Enemy attacks were often delivered by units of infantry crawling all the way to close assault positions. These Japs had their helmets bristling with grass and weeds. Often the first indication of an approaching attack would be when outposts spotted grassy helmets moving in the deep cogon grass. Our own men had elastic bands around their helmets for the purpose of inserting grass and twigs and often our defenses hesitated to fire as identification was difficult.

In no case was an enemy attack upon one of the perimeters of the 21st Infantry units successful. Flame throwers, and white phosphorous were particularly effective and literally made the Japs squeal.

Enemy infiltraters at night would cut telephone wire lines, and then wait in ambush for linemen to come to make repairs. Litter bearers and Aid Men drew particularly heavy fire.

Although the enemy used captured ordnance to supplement their own fire, his snipers used only Japanese rifles. This permitted our troops to detect their location because of the distinctive report.

The enemy used reverse slope defense tactics effectively. Every reverse slope in the area was well defended. Every foot of the terrain attacked was utilized properly for defense. His utilization of the terrain for defense was exceptionally good. All of his positions were mutually supporting. Most enemy fox holes were constructed in the shape of an inverted boot. His fire step and firing position toward us was in the toe. The deep heel was used to retire into for cover during our artillery and mortar fire. Enemy artillery pieces were located in covered emplacements well concealed with deep caves behind the gun for protection of gunners.

One of our officers, Lieutenant Anderson, who regained our lines after spending two days wounded inside enemy lines had an opportunity to observe enemy actions closely. All night was utilized for moving up ammunition and supplies by hand cart. He reported machine gun positions near draws and noses where the gun would be located on a forward slope. When artillery or mortar fire fell near the position the crews calmly went around the reverse side on a trail going around a nearby corner or curve to a protected reverse slope position. As soon as our fire ceased the gunners immediately re-occupied their positions.

In many cases our riflemen failed to dig their fox holes deep enough. During enemy mortar fire they were forced to crouch in their holes because the shallowness prevented them from standing upright. This lost them their observation completely and permitted the enemy to get up to bayonet range to where our riflemen was disadvantageously located to protect himself. Had he had a deep enough fox hole he could have remained erect and continued firing from cover and better protected himself from closely advancing enemy infantry men.

W. J. VERBECK,
Colonel, 21 Infantry,
Commanding.

HEADQUARTERS 21ST INFANTRY
Office of the Regimental Commander

A.P.O. # 24.
6 December 1944.

Subject: Commendation.

To   : Officers and Men of the 21st Infantry.

1. The 21st Infantry was committed to action against strong hostile forces at PINAMOPOAN, LEYTE ISLAND, PHILIPPINE ISLANDS, on 5 November 1944. The Commanding General, 24th Division directed: "The initiative will be maintained at all costs." From 5 November to 16 November at 1200, a period of twelve days, this order was carried out in continuous combat against a superior and determined hostile force. Every effort by the enemy to hold PINAMOPOAN RIDGE was made. Under conditions of difficult terrain, unfavorable weather, uncertain supply conditions and with no reinforcements the 21st Infantry ejected the enemy from PINAMOPOAN RIDGE. During the twelve day period 1779 of the enemy were killed.

2. It is with a feeling of deep pride that the undersigned commends the Officers and Men of the 21st Infantry for their achievement.

W. J. VERBECK,
Colonel, 21st Infantry,
Commanding.

Major Roy Marcy
in New Guinea

Captain Gerald Lockhart

DARO

The actual relief of the 21st Infantry from its positions on Breakneck Ridge occurred on 17 November 1944. The Regiment which thirteen days before had numbered 3050 now with a strength of less than 1600 officers and men returned to the vicinity of Jaro for rest and rehabilitation. However, the need for a deployed defense of the Western slopes of the Leyte Valley brought forth orders to occupy defensive positions. Long Toms were now bombarding Ormoc from the vicinity of Daro which was five miles west of Jaro. The 2nd and 3rd Battlions, therefore, moved out from Jaro on 18 November and occupied the hills around the guns. The 1st Battalion remained at Jaro. The rainy season on Leyte was now at its worst. Daro was cold and knee deep in mud. Our troops had neither blankets, dry clothes nor socks. Many were ill with dysentery, and immersion foot. It rained constantly. Further to the West in the high mountains were stationed one company from each of the two battalions. One company was on Mount Laao and one on Mount Mamban. Supplies and food bogged down on the muddy roads and trails. The veterans of Breakneck dug in and raised banana leaf roofs and waited. Mount Laao and Mamban were rough. We stayed here until 10 December.

CARIGARA

From 10 December to 26 December the Regiment moved to the North coast of Leyte to take up positions to defend the beach against enemy landing or raiding attempts. The First Battalion was deployed in the vicinity of Barugo, a pleasant town which had been left comparatively untouched by the War. The 1st Battalion was under the command of Major Lamar W. Little. The Second Battalion under command of Major Francis R. Dice and the Third under Lt.Col. Eric Ramee stretched from Carigara to Capoocan. Rest and rehabilitation took place. New clothing and equipment arrived and some replacements were received.

MINDORO

Elements of the 21st Infantry participated in a number of campaigns during the period 21 December 1944 to the 6th of March 1945. The 3rd Battalion under the command of Lt.Colonel Eric Ramee sailed for Mindoro on 21 December where attacks on the convoy at sea caused casualties and heavy loss of equipment. Landing at San Jose, Mindoro, this battalion was under constant air attack and withstood a naval bombardment by enemy battleships, cruisers and destroyers. The remainder of the regiment sailed from Leyte for Mindoro on 27 December. On the 28th the convoy was under bombing and Kamikaze attack all day and two ships of the convoy carrying munitions and gasoline were blown up with a loss of all aboard. No 21st Infantrymen however were lost. Other ships were also bombed and sunk and the regiment suffered some casualties. The Regiment landed on December 30th having been attacked and bombed all the trip. In defensive position the troops were subject to repeated air bombings until 7 January 1945.

In the first ten days of January 1945 elements of the 3rd Battalion successfully defeated enemy garrisons at Bongabong and Pinamalayan on Mindoro and at Boak on Marinduque Island. Company I under Captain Sothoron Able in two sharp fights brought Pinamalayan under our control while Lieutenant Milton E. Wilson with Company K surrounded the Jap garrison of Boak in a schoolhouse and killed them all.

MINDORO (cont.)

The liberation of Northern Mindoro was carried out by the 21st Infantry. Lt. Colonel Henderson acted as military governor and restored order and civil liberties among the peoples. In conjunction with a small guerrilla regiment under command of Major Ramon Ruffee, the 21st Infantry - less 1st Battalion which was at San Jose - moved overland from Pinamalayan toward Gusay, a Jap strong point, where it was reported that 400 enemy troops were concentrated. At the same time Company F under command of Captain Charles R. Jameson, Jr., moved by water in commandeered sail boats to Najuan. I Company guarded Pinamalayan. K Company was still at Boak in Marinduque Island. The 2nd Battalion (less F. Company) surprised and dispersed the enemy at Gusay on January 19-20. On the evening of 19 January a Japanese patrol was ambushed by Regimental Headquarters personnel in the Regimental Command Post where they had walked without knowing that the 2nd Battalion was surrounding their own base at Gusay. The 2nd Battalion had just completed a four day march from Pinamalayan through the mountains with only carometas and ponies and buffalo carts for transportation. Regimental C.P. and Headquarters company had accompanied the 2nd Battalion. During this march two rivers were crossed on parts of bridges destroyed by the enemy's delaying forces. Every item of equipment including about 3000 rounds of 81m.m. mortar ammunition was manhandled across the river. Only one Jap escaped alive from the ambush in the Rgt. C.P. 81m.m. mortars immediately fired on Gusay with good results.

Company F, disembarked because of unfavorable winds and finally completed a gruelling march to Najuan on foot in time to cut off the enemy's withdrawal from Gusay towards Calipan, the capitol.

Captain Kermit Blaney was in command of L. Company which spearheaded the 3rd Battalion's (-) thrust to take Calipan. There were sharp fights at Km. 8, Km. 7, and Km. 6. The guerrillas participated in this fighting of 23 January. On the 24th the 21st entered the capitol without opposition and the enemy withdrew to the hills to the West. We rested in and around Calipan and first tasted the joys of being entertained by a liberated people. Food was good for awhile. There also was Calipan gin.

In San Jose a regimental area and camp was established, badly needed replacements were received, equipment and clothes were replaced and a period of rehabilitation and training was started.

DIPOLOG

During the last days of March 1945 a force of one division was assembled for the capture of Zamboanga in Southwest Mindanao. Just prior to the amphibious assault, the air attacks against the enemy in Zamboanga were stepped up. Marine air group 24 had landed at Dipolog on the Northwestern coast of the Zamboanga Penninsula. They were using the Point as a base of operations as it was in the hands of friendly Filipino guerrillas. Information was received that an enemy force of about 400 was advancing from the interior to capture Dipolog. Accordingly two companies of the 2nd Battalion, 21st Infantry were flown to Dipolog from Mindoro in transport planes. This airborne force secured the air base and the town and the hostile force turned back. This was the first landing of ground forces on Mindanao.

LATRINE IN MINDORO

On a gas drum in Mondoro,
In a field of cogon grass
You get seated on the furnace,
And slowly fry your

The thing's not made for softness,
And the seat's not laquered green.
There's no solid Chick Sales comfort,
If you get just what I mean.

As the ants crawl up your backbone,
The sweat rolls down your leg.
You feel the sunbaked drumhead
Hot enough to boil an egg.

Now it jams your cheeks together
Now it crimps the skin below.
And the sand blows up the seathole,
As the sultry breezes blow.

When the hole's too big to fit you,
And you slide inside the drum.
You must gently use your tissue
Lest you amputate your thumb.

When the detail is finished burning,
Hot oil smokes right through your thighs,
Or you grope for paper blindly
As the lime blows in your eyes.

In the mornings of the future,
When you answer nature's call.
You'll not forget that oil drum -
Inside the burlap wall.

Signboard at Entrance to "Gimlets Grove"

Sam Jose, Mindoro

THE BEER RATION

Having a warm bottle of beer at Sleepy Hollow at Gimlet's Grove, San Jose, Mindoro.

Left to Right: Col. Verbeck, Lieut. Seyle, Capt. Allen, Major Coers, Major Sloan, Capt. Aitken, Lieut. Col. Henderson, Chaplain Cashman.

March 1945.

Good Morning, Sir. You Got Dirty Clothes?

Leyte

Tropical Shower — Mindora

MINDORO CAMPAIGN

When to Gusay we went hiking
Toward the rain belt we were striking,
And the caratella carts were quite a few.
But the streams were high and muddy,
And let me tell you buddy-
That the blasted bridges made the doughboys blue.

Well, we climbed the blasted mountain,
While the clouds burst like a fountain,
And the mortar ammunition sure was tough.
So the ponies fell behind us
And the task force couldn't find us,
Believe me, 10 KM per day was quite enough.

Now, an old man and his daughter
Led the Jappies to their slaughter,
And they wandered into camp without a qualm.
So entirely unsuspecting
In a close group all collecting,
While our men were hiding, waiting, cool and calm.

With all guns and weapons blazing,
The slaughter was amazing
And we fired enough munitions for a day.
When the nips stopped kicking,
For gadgets we went picking-
But you ought to see the one that got away.

The Regimental Surgeon
Without a bit of urgin'
Climbed a nipa shack and in it found an egg.
But when Verbeck started dining,
The bullets they came whining
And it made the frightened couple shake a leg.

Tojo took it on the lam,
From the town of Calipan,
And we occupied the place in time for dinner.

Now we'll sit right here and squat
'Cause the weather's getting hot
From the looks of things we're sure to get no thinner.

GUERILLA REPORTS

The Japanese force defending Northern Mindoro was driven from Calipan on 23 January 1945 and scattered towards the mountains to the West. For the next week the Regiment of Mindoro guerrillas under command of Major Ramon Ruffee carried out a campaign to finish off the defeated Jap force. These Filipino troops had greatly assisted the 21st Infantry in its Mindoro Campaign. Now, reinforced by mortar and machine gun units from the 2nd and 3rd Battalions, 21st Infantry, they tackled the enemy in the hills.

Two sample accounts of guerrilla actions follow:

PHILLIPINE ARMY
BOLO AREA

29 January, 1945

SUBJECT: Encounter with the Japs, report on
TO : CO, Bolo Area

On Jan. 25, 1945, Lt. I. Minay with twenty four (24) armed men, Sgt. Aploinar with eleven (11) armed men and the Trench Mortar Section of eleven (11) men all under my direct command proceeded to Katuwiran to establish our line of attack.

At 6:00 AM the next day, Jan. 26, 1945 I sent patrol out to verify enemy positions. Within 25 minutes the patrol arrived reporting that the Japs were concentrated at Longos foot Bridge and among the houses within the vicinity.

I ordered Lt. I. Minay and Sgt. Flores to deploy the men one hundred yards ahead of the Trench Mortar, before I ordered the Mortar Men to fire.

Exactly at 8:00 AM the pounding of the Trench Mortar began at the place where the Japs were concentrated. On the first concentration of fire the Japs were at once demoralized and they were all scattered around. My men were able to advance as far as 25 yard from the enemy positions. We saw most of them already armless. In our first encounter the Japs retreated and I ordered all men to advance to gain the positions of the Japs. We were on failure because of the heavy machine-gun fire concentrated to the place where we deployed. The Japs have one (1) .50 cal. MG, and two (2) .30 cal. MG with several sub-machine guns in operation. I ordered the men to hold the line. For about three hours heavy exchange of fire was made. On this first encounter of ours the men on the front estimated that they were able to kill twenty (20) plus. We could see those armless Japs taking rifles from the dead ones. The firing of the Japs lasted for two hours.

At 2:00 PM I ordered a concentration of Mortar fire to the place where we spotted the machine gun emplacements. The Japs did not answer our fire. After 30 minutes, we heard the Japs firing at our right and left flanks, while the machine guns began to fire again at our front covering their advance to our line of resistance. Still the boys held the line. The boys were able to kill lots in their advance for they advance on an open field. Fearing that we might be encircled I ordered my men to withdraw to our first line of attack and hold the line again. The machine-gun fire lasted for two hours. Little by little we retreated to the other side of the river.

In my supposition all in all we were able to kill forty (40) Japs. We still saw blood scattered around on their fox-holes and along their ways of retreat, when we attack them last 28 Jan. '45. We have captured one (1) box of ammunitions .30 cal. Japs machine gun, one (1) rifle .25 cal. and several magazines of .50 and .30 cals. machine guns.

The Japs left plenty of ammunitions on the field. They have wasted most of their ammunitions during our combat.

/s/ RAMON ANONUEVO
1st Lieut., Inf.
CO "C" Co

PHILIPPINE ARMY
BOLO AREA

29 Jan. '45

SUBJECT: Combat report (Longos Campaign)
TO : CO, Bolo Area

1. The following combat reports in Longos against the enemy are hereby submitted.

   2. a. STRENGTH OF OUR UNIT — Five (5) Officers and one hundred fourteen (114) enlisted men.

      b. NUMBER OF ARMS ——————— One hundred seventeen (117) rifles and two (2) Trench Mortars 81 MM.

      c. OFFICER IN CHARGE ——— Lt. DOMINADOR B. ADEVA, Inf
        OFFICERS WHO PARTICIPATED - Lts. ANONUEVO, GIMENEZ, BACARRO & MINAY.

      d. CASUALTY SUSTAINED ————— NONE

      e. BOOTY TAKEN ——————————— AMMUNITION, RICE and considerable Japanese Army Supply.

      f. SUPPLY ———————————————— Furnished by Civilians

   3. ENEMY STRENGTH ——————— Three hundred to four hundred (300 - 400) including officers.

      b. Number of Arms——————— Estimated to be two hundred (200) including rifles and machine guns.

      c. SUPPLY ——————————————— The Japs had considerable number of rice and cattle taken forcibly from civilians.

    d. ENEMY DISPOSITION --   All Along the road from Longos to Calabugao. Entrenchment had been established all along these points.

    e. NAME OF OFFICER ----   UNKNOWN

    f. CASUALTIES SUSTAINED-   Estimated to be from forty (40) to fifty (50) men.

4. NARRATIVE REPORT ----- The enemy composed mostly of those who retreated from GUSAY and CALAPAN were entrenched all along the road from Longos River to Calabugao northward. They numbered approximately from three hundred (300) to 400 men including Officers. Machine gun emplacements were established in their barracks covering the road in the East side. They were evidently ready for any attack as Japs had been observed entrenched in their fox-hole day and night. In the morning of Jan. 28, '45 my men and four (4) officers and one hundred fourteen (114) enlisted men after receiving instructions from me disposed themselves along the East and South sides of the enemy positions. At zero "hour" has been announced; the signal which, will be the pounding of the Trench Mortar to the enemy positions, followed by two (2) smoke shells. The last two (2) smoke shells served as the "zero" hour and for the men to jump in the enemy.

At nine (9:00 AM) of the same day the pounding commenced, and after one half hour, of pounding, the signal for the whole unit was delivered. Our men at a double quick, but cautiously approached the enemy position. Enemy were seen dislodged from their entrenchment and were subjected to our rifle firing. The enemy was not able to effect any firing as they were all in panic, caused principally by the acute firing of the Trench Mortar and the traversing rapid firing of our men. However, their main force were able to "take off" for the mountain located in the West side of their position. Our men got hold of their positions taking as enemy booty, ammunitions, gas mask, rain coats, rice and meat. Scouts were immediately dispatched within the vicinity but discovered no enemy. However, foot-prints were discovered, presumably Japanese, leading to the mountain.

We stayed in the place until late in the afternoon, when I received reports that the enemy was somewhere in the mountain, two and a half kilometers from our position, which was within a Trench Mortar range. Immediately I ordered a twenty minutes pounding in the direction specified, with all the ammunitions left. An hour later report was received that the enemy in that area was again in turmoil. American lone plane was also observed encircling within the enemy area dropping several small explosions, which to my estimation were hand grenades. *

The complete detail regarding enemy casualties is still in the process, as our S-2 Officer with his personnel are out in that area for more information. More reports will follow.

                                              /s/ DOMINADOR B. ADEVA
                                                   1st Lieut., Inf
                                              In-charge of Operation.

* Regimental Commander, 21st Infantry, observing the action in a L-5 observation plane.

Bridge expedient constructed by 2nd Bn during the Pinamalayan - Calapan Mindoro, P. I. campaign. January 18, 1945

GO 68

General Orders)
No. 68)

WAR DEPARTMENT
Washington 25, D.C., 14 August 1945.

BATTLE HONORS.—As authorized by Executive Order 9396 (sec. I, WD Bul. 22, 1943), superseding Executive Order 9075 (sec. IIII, WD Bul. 11, 1942), citations of the following units in the general orders indicated are confirmed under the provisions of section IV, WD Circular 333, 1943, in the name of the President of the United States as public evidence of deserved honor and distinction:

* * *

19. CANNON COMPANY, 21ST INFANTRY REGIMENT, is cited for outstanding heroism and gallantry in supporting the drive of an airborne division from Nasugbu to Manila, Philippine Islands, 31 January to 5 February 1945. On 31 January the Cannon Company, 21st Infantry Regiment, landed at Nasugbu, Luzon. It was the only armored unit in support of the airborne division at that time. When heavy enemy resistance was encountered at Cayungan on 1 February, this company moved forward under hostile artillery and automatic weapons fire to cover the advance of leading units across a deep ravine. By direct fire, promptly and accurately placed, this company neutralized enemy automatic weapons permitting the seizure of the position with minimum losses to our forces. On 2 February at Aga the division advance was held up by another strongpoint. Despite the fact that its vehicles drew heavy hostile artillery, mortar, and automatic fire, this company advanced rapidly to forward positions and again by direct fire neutralized the enemy position. On 3 February, during the advance on Tagaytay Ridge, from an area subject to enemy artillery, mortar, and small-arms fire, the Cannon Company, 21st Infantry Regiment, delivered direct fire on enemy emplacements, greatly facilitating the seizure of the area. On 4 February, with assault units of the division, this company surprised and destroyed hostile groups in four stone houses guarding approaches to the Imus River Bridge. This action enabled the mined structure to be secured before it could be destroyed. By aggressive action at Las Pinas the same day, the self-propelled mounts reduced pillboxes near the Las Pinas Bridge, permitting this bridge, also mined, to be secured before the charges could be detonated. Capturing these two bridges intact was of greatest importance to the 31-mile advance made by the division that day. At Paranaque 5 February, encountering main defenses of the heavily fortified Genko Line guarding approaches to Manila and Nichols Field, the company pushed through streets covered by hostile artillery and antitank guns and mined with 250 KG aerial bombs, destroyed numerous pillboxes and large roadblocks, and materially aided the breaching of outer defenses. Throughout this entire series of actions, the Cannon Company, 21st Infantry Regiment, subordinated personal safety to aggressive action despite heavy casualties, and by its gallant action earned the admiration of all units it had supported. (General Orders 69, Headquarters, Eighth Army, 25 June 1945, as approved by the Commander in Chief, United States Army Forces, Pacific.)

* * * *

By order of the Secretary of War:

G. C. MARSHALL,
Chief of Staff

Official:
EDWARD F. WITSELL
Major General
Acting The Adjutant General

In the Luzon campaign from 31 January 1945 to 3 March 1945, the Cannon Company, 21st Infantry, attached to the 11th Airborne Division, participated in the following engagements: Nasugbu, Wawa, Lian, Tagaytay, Imus, Paranaque, Zapote, Las Pinas, Nichols Field, Fort William McKinley, Alabang and Los Banos. During this campaign four out of their eight self-propelled mounts were destroyed in action. The Company suffered heavy casualties among them the Company Commander, Captain Harold Edleson, killed.

LUBANG

The First Battalion now commanded by Major Nicholas Sloan conducted a rapid campaign on another island. Previous reconnaissances had been made by scouting parties under command of Lieut. Philip Irons and Lieut. Thomas R. Campbell. Twenty-four hours prior to the main landing of the First Battalion, a force under command of Lt. Campbell landed on Lubang and a road block was established to cut off enemy retreat into the jungle hinterland. Then Campbell with another small force attacked an enemy garrison in the capitol city of Lubang and killed several on the night of 28 February - 1 March. He was in radio communication with the landing force. Sloan's men made an amphibious landing after a naval bombardment at the town of Tilic on Lubang Island. At the same time Campbell's force approached Tilic to help the landing force. After securing Tilic, Sloan's battalion pushed the enemy into the hills where after receiving some losses in a sharp encounter dispersed and destroyed the enemy force of 200 or more. The entire action lasted from 1 March until 6 March. The battalion then returned to San Jose.

The Commanding Officer, 21st Infantry, received his third wound of the war at Lubang. The regimental S-3, Captain Gerald Lockhart who was wounded at Hollandia and again at Hill 1525, conceeds first place in radio communication from Mindoro.

WAR DEPARTMENT
MESSAGEFORM

Date 3 March 45

File No. _____
Office of origin DIAMOND 6
Telephone No. _____

(Arm or service)   (Division)   (Branch)   (Section)   (Symbol)

Address SAN JOSE MINDORO

To:
COMMANDING OFFICER
21st INFANTRY
DIAMOND RED 6

WIRE OR RADIO	PRECEDENCE	ESSENTIAL MILITARY MAIL
Urgent		Air mail
Priority		Special delivery
Routine	X	Ordinary
Deferred		Registered
Week end		

Any message not X'd for precedence will be sent "Deferred."

Initial of officer assigning precedence

MESSAGE:

YOU WON X CONGRATULATIONS FROM THE STAFF

ESPECIALLY FROM LOCKHART END

111

BRONZE STAR

Captain KERMIT B. BLANEY, Infantry, United States Army. For meritorious achievement in connection with military operations against the enemy in the Philippine Islands from 22 January to 15 May 1945. During the Northeast Mindoro Campaign at Km 8, Km 7 and Km 6 south of Calipan, Captain Blaney was company commander of a rifle company which was assault company of a battalion of infantry attacking toward Calipan. In a steady advance against continuous enemy automatic weapons defensive positions Captain Blaney showed great ability and personal courage in maintaining aggressive advance and defeating the last enemy defenses south of Calipan. From 3 May to 15 May 1945 during the Mindanao Campaign, Captain Blaney a rifle company commander, led his company continuously throughout the period in daily attacks. His ability and outstanding leadership were considered to be a great asset in maintenance of the initiative during this period when casualties were very high. Captain Blaney was withdrawn from combat on 15 May upon division order for temporary duty in the United States.

BRONZE STAR

Captain (then First Lieutenant) PHILIP S. IRONS, III, Infantry, United States Army. For meritorious achievement in connection with military operations against the enemy at Lubang, Philippine Islands from 16 to 17 February 1945. Captain Irons was leader of a reconnaissance patrol consisting of two officers and three enlisted men which landed on enemy-held Lubang Island prior to the main operation. It was the mission of this patrol to determine the location, strength and general condition of the Japanese garrison. Captain Irons and his men were brought to within a mile of the island by PT Boat at night. From this point they rowed to shore in small rubber boats. Armed only with rifles, grenades and submachine guns the men stepped ashore, concealed their rubber boats, and moved cautiously up the beach. Since reconnaissance was impossible in the darkness they found a sheltered spot and slept until daylight. The following morning Captain Irons led his men inland. In reconnoitering over exceedingly rough terrain through enemy territory he took his men to the crest of a twenty-six hundred foot hill commanding the island. From here he was able to observe enemy installations for an entire day carefully noting roads and bridges and drawing sketches of the terrain features. Throughout the two-day mission Captain Irons displayed outstanding leadership, resourcefulness and courage under the constant danger of discovery by the enemy. The information he obtained was of great value in planning the subsequent operation which was carried out successfully with a minimum loss of life and time. Captain Iron's heroic devotion to duty and disregard for his personal safety reflect great credit upon himself and the military service.

BRONZE STAR

Private JOAQUIN R. TAPIA, Infantry, United States Army. For heroic achievement in connection with military operations against the enemy at Lubang, Philippine Islands, on 2 March 1945. Private Tapia volunteered to join a patrol of four members to reconnoiter at night in advance of our own front lines to locate enemy machine gun postions and to rescue any living from four of our men who were missing from the afternoon's action. During this operation Private Tapia was killed. Private Tapia's total disregard for his own personal safety was a source of inspiration to all members of the patrol and reflects great credit upon himself and the military service.

Capt. James M. Parent
C.O. Co. G, Wounded Mindanao

Capt. Kermit Blaney
Commander of "Love" Company

Capt. Sothoron K. Able
Who Commanded I Company on Mindoro and Mindanao. Able was seriously wounded on Mindanao.

ROSTER OF OFFICERS, 21ST INFANTRY, 10 March 1945.

COLONEL
Verbeck, William J. — Regt'l Commander

LT COLONELS
Henderson, Arthur H., — Regt'l Ex O., (SC)
Ramee, Eric P., — Comdg 3rd Bn., (SC) (Lv U.S.)

MAJORS
Dice, Francis R., — Regt'l S-2, (SC)
Bussell, Frank T., — Regt'l Supply O, (S-4) (Lv U.S.)
Marcy, Roy W., — Comdg 2nd Bn. (SC)
Suber, Tom W., — 3rd, Bn, Ex O., (SC)
Sloan, Nicholas E., — Comdg 1st Bn., (SC)

CAPTAINS
Stanford, Don D., — Hq Co 3rd Bn, Hq Co Comdr, (Bn S-1)
Girardeau, John H., Jr., — Ex O, 1st Bn.
Kelley, Jack H., — Ex O, 2nd Bn.
Lockhart, Gerald L., — Regt'l S-3, Regt'l Opns O.
Thompson, James H., — Hq Co 2nd Bn, Hq Co Comdr, (Bn S-1)
Jameson, Charles R., Jr., — Comdg Co "F"
Childs, John A. — Comdg Co "C"
Aitken, Malcolm D., — Hq Co 1st Bn, Hq Co Comdr, (Bn S-1)
Williams, Jay B., Jr., — Hq Co 3rd Bn, Bn S-3, Bn Opns O.
Becker, Philip A., — Pers Adj, Ass't Adj, Bond & Ins O.
Candler, Eugene N. — Comdg Hq Co. (Lv U.S.)
Allen, Shelton P., — Regt'l Munn O., Actg Regt'l S-4
Reid, Neil D. — Comdg Co "M"
Olson, Erwin L., — Comdg Serv Co, Unit Loading O.
Brown, Robert A. — Regt'l S-1, Regt'l Claims O.
Kilgo, Robert L., — Comdg Co "E"
Able, Sothoron K. — Comdg Co "I"
Blaney, Kermit B. — Comdg Co "L"
Vienneau, Ernest L., — Comdg Co "K"
Wicker, Glenes E., — Comdg A-T Co
Ender, Robert R., — Comdg Co "H"
Mayer, John D., — 2nd Bn Hq., Bn S-3, Bn Opns O. (Lv U.S.)
Haywood, Major G. — Regt'l MTO, Serv Co
Curles, Cecil M., — Comdg Cannon Co

CAPTAINS, MC, DC, CH.
Coers, Burt N.,........Major... — Regt'l Surgeon, (MC) (Lv U.S.)
Berkowitz, Julius — Regt'l Dental Surgeon, (DC)
Jones, Erner — 2nd Bn Surgeon (MC) (Actg Regt'l Surg.)
Mutziger, Dudley H., — 2nd Bn Surgeon (MC)
Cashman, Malachy, J.P., — Regt'l Chaplain (CH)
Luria, Sidney B., — 3rd Bn Surgeon (MC)
Walters, Murray M., — Ass't Regt'l Chaplain (CH) (Hosp)
Rhein, William L., — Ass't Regt'l Dental Surg., (DC)
Cathcart, John W., — 1st Bn Surgeon (MC)

1st LIEUTENANT
Parent, James M., — Comdg Co "G"
Hash, Russell T., — Co "C"
Farmer, Edward S., — 1st Bn Hq, Bn S-3, Bn Opns O.
Mote, Jack A., — 3rd Bn Hq Co, Bn MTO, (Lv U.S.)
Moore, Dan C., — Co "H"

1ST LIEUTENANTS (cont.)

Farrell, John B.,	2nd Bn Hq Co.
Freeman, Coleman R.,	A-T Co, (Lv U.S.)
Goldpaugh, John J.,	Co "M"
Sullivan, John C.,	Co "F" (Atch Unasgned)
McNamara, Warren M.,	Comdg Co "D"
Malone, Robert H.,	Comdg Co "A"
Miller, George J.,	Co "E"
Dantzler, LeRoy A., Jr.,	A-T Co
Seyle, Frank W.,	Regt'l Gas & Cam O.
Stewart, Alvin E.,	Co "F"
Stimson, Arthur E.,	Regt'l Liaison O, Custodian of Classified Documents.
Trembley, Arthur N., Jr.,	Co "D"
Oler, William L.,	Co "L"
Corbishley, Sidney F.,	Serv Co, Regt'l MMO
Trammell, Alonzo K.,	Hq Co, 2nd Bn
Boyd, Wilbur B.,	Co "I"
Sicely, Maruice F.,	Co "E"
Smith, Hobert P.,	Co "F"
Hammar, Frank W.,	Co "G"
Lannin, Thomas R.,	Co "E" (DS 24th Div)
Williams, Herbert Jr.,	3rd Bn Hq Co., Bn Comm O.
Kirkpatrick, Earl R.,	2nd Bn, Hq Co
Smith, John H.,	Co "A"
Margolis, Robert J.,	Co "C"
Nelson, Vernon R.,	Co "K"
Small, Jack	2nd Bn Hq Co, Bn Comm O.
St Clair, Robert J.,	Co "B"
Sundquist, Raymound M.,	Hq Co
Wiegand, Allen W.,	1st Bn Hq Co, Bn Comm O.
Fosse, Maurice J.,	Co "D"
Snyder, Henry A.,	Cannon Co.
Wisor, Robert L.,	Co "D"
Doyel, James T., Jr.,	1st Bn Hq Co Bn MTO
Wilsey, Clarence R.,	Co "H"
Camp, Paul B.,	A-T Co
Cassel, Robert F.,	Cannon Co
Corrigan, Michael J.,	Regt'l Ass't S-3, I & E O.
Counts, Charles R.,	Co "C"
Crouch, Theodore	Comdg Co "B"
Hall, Claude H.,	Co "F" (D.S. 24th Div, G-4)
Irons, Philip S., III,	1st Bn, Bn S-2
Longridge, Kermit C.,	A-T Co
Morgan, Norman O.,	Cannon Co
Wilson, Milton E.,	Co "K"
Bland, Irvin G.,	Co "I"
Froome, James N., Jr.,	Regt'l Hq Co, Regt'l Comm O
Hammer, Richard P.,	Co "H" (Lv U.S.)
Kester, Alfred J.,	3rd Bn Hq Co, (Hosp)
Langford, William M.,	Co "D"
Lemm, Stanley C.,	2nd Bn, Bn S-4, Bn Fire Marshal, Serv Co
Lesky, Albert W.,	Co "G"
Murphy, James F.,	A-T Co
Patrick, William J.,	3rd Bn, Bn S-4, Bn Fire Marshal, Serv Co
Sabatine, Matthew	1st Bn, Bn S-4, Bn Fire Marshal, Serv Co
Young, Emmitte E.,	3rd Bn Hq Co

Van De Riet, Harry J.,	Co "A" (Lv U.S.)
Bemis, Russell B.,	Serv Co, Ass't S-4 (Hosp)
O'Hara, James M.,	3rd Bn Hq Co
McKeon, Robert G.,	2nd Bn Hq, Bn S-2
Routen, Eugene V.,	Co "E"
Henebery, John J., Jr.,	Co "H"
Hudson, Roger W.,	Regt'l Liaison O.
Marquez, Thomas	Co "G"
Campbell, Thomas R.,	Co "C"
Bunkley, Thomas H.,	Co "M"
Hartman, William H.,	Co "B" (Hosp)
Buttice, Angelo P.,	Co "B"

1st LIEUTENANTS, MC, DC, CH.

Klann, Herman R.,	Ass't Regt'l Chaplain, (CH)
Chukur, Vincent J.,.....2nd Lt...	Ass't Regt'l Surgeon, (MAC)

2nd LIEUTENANTS

Didak, Eugene J.,	Co "E" (Hosp)
Eddy, Lowell P.,	A-T Co
Ford, Clarence R.,	Co "F"
Steinberger, Joseph G.,	Co "I"
Smith, Arthur C.,	SSO, Postal O, Asst S-1, (Serv Co)
Battin, Donald H.,	Serv Co, Ass't Adj.
Morton, Stuart C.,	Co "G"
Carmody, Robert J.,	Co "A"
Mullis, Jack R.,	1st Bn Hq Co
Reifsnyder, Henry G., Jr.,	Co "H"
Ryan, Donald H.,	Co "L"
Lehrer, Joseph A.,	3rd Bn Hq, Bn S-2
Runciman, Alexander P.,	Co "I"
Levine, Solomon	Co "L"
Prickett, Loyd L.,	Co "K"
Nacheff, Steve P.,	Ass't S-4, Serv Co. (Lv U.S.)
Proctor, Harold I.,	Co "L" (Hosp)
Fittz, Samuel C.,	Co "E"
Grevie, Peter W.,	Co "D"
Hamby, Paul W.,	Co "K"
Whalen, John C.,	Co "K"
Munson, Frank W.,	Co "M"
O'Brian, Donald A.,	Co "G"
Lostroch, Elwood, L.,	Hq Co, (DS 24th Div)
Procento, Anthony	Co "B" (Hosp)
McConnell, Paul E.,	1st Bn Hq Co
Roberts, Harris K.,	Co "C"
Massar, George D.,	Co "H"
Martin, Clarence A., Jr.,	Co "F"

WARRANT OFFICERS J.G.

Lancaster, James L.,	Ass't Regt'l S-1 (Lv U.S.)
Evans, Roy A.,	Ass't Munn O., (Lv U.S.)

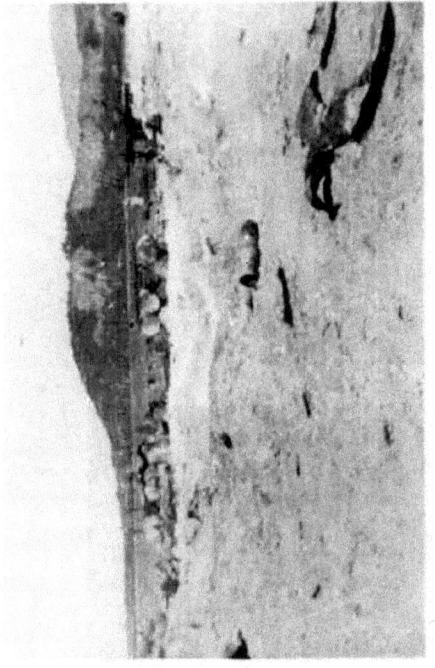

Tilic, Lubang, P.I. destroyed by navy shelling while preparing for 1st Bn landing

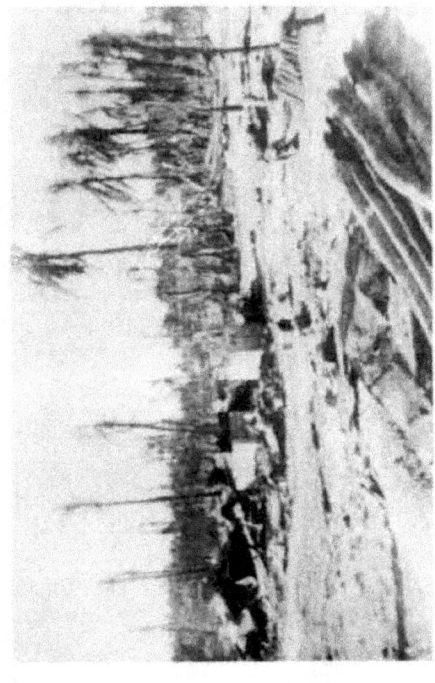

Jap oil dump blown up by naval shelling at Tilic, Lubang, P.I.

Jap "Q" Boats at Tilic, Lubang, P.I.

Tilic, Lubang Island, P.I. on fire from Naval Shelling during preparation for 1st Bn's 21st Infantry landing March 1945.

Lieut. Col. Arthur Henderson
Regimental Executive Officer
at Mindoro and Mindanao.

Major Erner Jones
Regimental Surgeon, Mindanao.

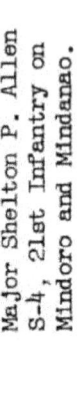

Major Shelton P. Allen
S-4, 21st Infantry on
Mindoro and Mindanao.

Capt. Bob Ender
C.O. Co. H.

Capt. Charles R. Jameson
C.O Company "Fox" on Leyte and Mindoro.

NEW YORK HERALD TRIBUNE, THURSDAY, APRIL 19, 1945

U.S. Units Land On Mindanao's Southwest Side

Seize 35-Mile Beachhead, Link Up With Guerrillas Are Threatening Davao

By Frank Kelley
By Wireless to the Herald Tribune
Copyright 1945, New York Tribune Inc.

ON BOARD FLAGSHIP OF ADMIRAL NOBLE OFF PARANG, Mindanao, Philippines, April 17 (Delayed).—In a major thrust that threatened the Japanese stronghold of Davao, on Mindanao Island, the American 24th Infantry Division landed without opposition this morning at two points one the eastern shore of Moro Gulf, Tous Island, in Ilana Bay, 100 air-line miles west of Davao and about the same distance east a half southward to occupy strategic Malabang airfield, seizure of of American-held Zamboanga.

General Douglas MacArthur's communique said that American troops had linked up with guerrilla forces and secured a thirty-five-mile-wide beachhead.

Waves of green-clad doughboys under the command of Colonel Thomas E. Clifford, of Covington, Va., who was an all-American football player for West Point in 1932, '34 and '35, hit the beach, beginning at 9 a.m., at the small coastal town of Parang.

Not a shot was fired at them from burning, flattened Parang, where the Japanese in April 1942, had put 4,000 men ashore, likewise without resistance, in their push toward Davao.

An hour earlier Colonel William J. Verbeck, of Manlius, N.Y., took other elements of the 24th ashore with aviation engineers twenty-one miles to the northwest behind Parang beachhead and near the delta of the Mindanao River. This force fanned out swiftly a mile and

tegic Malabang airfield, seizure of which last Thursday by guerrillas wrested one of the best strips on Mindanao from the enemy.

Malabang airfield, developed by the American Army before the war and improved by the Japanese has two runways, one 7,500 feet long and the other 4,500 feet long. The surface is of well-packed volcanic ash and could take Superfortresses if necessary.

Spotter planes from our supporting cruisers and destroyers flew twelve miles up the Mindanao River this morning and reported the American flag flying from a pole. Natives were waving to the planes. Native sailboats were on the river, and there was no sign of enemy activity on the roads in the area.

Cotabato, a town of 8,000 population ten miles south of the Mindanao River, was bombed by two waves of 13th Air Force Liberators as the troops approached the beach.

Within an hour of landing Lieutenant General Robert L. Eichelberger, commanding the 8th Army, left a cruiser to go ashore. With him went Major General Franklin C. Sibert, of Destin, Fla., commanding the 10th Corps, which is in operational control of the beachhead, and Major General Roscoe B. Woodruff, of San Antonio, Tex., commanding the 24th Division.

Sibert and Woodruff are veterans of Leyte, Sibert having directed the same corps in the northern sector. From Leyte units of the 24th were assigned to assault Mindoro, Marinduque, Corregidor, Lubang, Verde, Simara and Rombion Islands.

Col. Verbeck and Major Nick Sloan
C.O. 1st Battalion on Lubang and Mindanao

Lieut. Col. Roy (Pappy) Marcy
C.O. 2nd Battalion on Mindanao

Lieut. Col. Tom Suber
C.O. 3rd Battalion until he was
seriously wounded on Mindanao

Excerpt from
"THEIR LAST STRONGHOLD"

A narrative account of
THE 24TH INFANTRY DIVISION

on

MINDANAO

by Major General R. B. Woodruff

HEADQUARTERS EIGHTH ARMY, APO 343, 24 May 1945.

TO: Commanding General, 24th Infantry Division, APO 24.

The lighting advance Mindanao and the courageous fighting in the Davao area have added new laurels to the already distinguished record of the 24th Division. The courage and skill of officers and men defeated a determined enemy on ground of his own choosing and has opened the way to a rapid completion of the destruction of Japanese forces on Mindanao. My warmest congratulations to the 24th Infantry Division upon the attainment of this objective.

R. L. EICHELBERGER,
Lieutenant General, USA,
Commanding.

I

MORO GULF TO DAVAO

The distance and pace of the 24th Infantry Division's thrust from Moro Gulf to Davao stand as a unique achievement in tropical warfare. Despite sporadic resistance, scores of destroyed bridges, roadblocks, ambushes and innumerable mines, the infantry spearheads traversed 140 road miles in 17 days, ending this assault march with the capture of Davao.

In less than three months of campaigning the division broke Nippon's last bastion in the Philippines, killing 7,000 of the enemy.

Davao was the oldest center of Japanese colonization in the Philippines, subjected to Nipponese penetration for almost thirty years. The city's 19,000 most influential citizens were Japs. During the planning stage of the campaign, Intelligence estimated that 36,000 enemy troops held Mindanao. Of these, 18,000 were reported in the Davao area --- the last strong concentration of Japanese forces in the Philippines. The enemy had had three years in which to prepare against the inevitable attack. He was well prepared. He expected the invasion to come from the sea, directly on Davao. Most of his guns faced Davao Gulf. Our overland backdoor attack caught him "with his pants down".

The division's assault march and the bitter fighting which followed moved through every kind of tropical terrain; fertile valleys and ridge-studded jungles, swamps and tortuous mountain passes, rich abaca and coconut plains, saltwater expanses and swift flowing rivers, country populated by a conglomeration of Christian Filipinos, Mohammedan Moros, and heathen savages.

Large sections of Mindanao's rain forests have never been explored by white men. Mountain chains, dominated by Mt. Apo (9,692 feet), follow a general north-south course through the island. The broad lower courses of the Mindanao River proved to be an asset to the division's assault, but the gorges of the upper Davao and Tolomo Rivers in the wild hinterland of Davao constituted the most difficult fighting terrain of the campaign.

The invasion plan called for a landing in force on the shores of Moro Gulf and the seizure of Malabang Airstrip, one of the largest and best on the island; then for a bold drive across the island via Highway #1, the "National Highway", which runs cross-island to Digos on Davao Gulf, thence north along the coast to Davao City.

Thirty six hours before the scheduled assault, information was received that Malabang Drome had been seized by guerrilla forces. Major General Franklin Sibert, commanding the X Corps, therefore directed that the initial landing be made at Parang. This required a change in Division plans while the convoy still sailed the high seas.

At 0800, 17 April 1945, the 3d Battalion, 21st Infantry landed at Baras and secured Malabang Strip and town. While the 34th Infantry Regiment remained a "floating reserve", a naval bombardment pounded Parang. Fourteen hundred high explosive shells were hurled against the narrow landing area, followed by a rocket barrage.

At 0900, the first wave of the 19th Infantry Regiment hit the beach at Parang. While one battalion secured the beachhead against light resistance, another pushed rapidly down Highway #1.

A 240-foot bridge across the Ambul River had been burned. The spearhead forded the shoulder-deep river, carrying all weapons and equipment, and secured high ground four miles south-east of Parang. By 1330, the 21st RCT had come ashore, followed by the 13th Field Artillery Battalion, and drove south. Overwater reconnaissance from Parang to the estuary of the Mindanao River fell to the 24th Cavalry Reconnaissance Troop. By the end of the first day a 35-mile strip of the coast was in American hands.

Though the Division Commander stepped into a spider hole and emerged with cracked ribs, Colonel William J. Verbeck, in command of the 21st Infantry, became the first casualty of the invasion. The Colonel was washing his face in a helmet and ducked for a final rinse when a sniper fired. The slug tore across his back. A burst from the submachinegun of an alert driver toppled the Jap out of a building twenty-five yards away. This was the third and last Jap killed during that day.

Push to Pikit

At dawn, 18 April, the 19th RCT commenced the drive toward the important road-and-river junction of Fort Pikit, an old American installation. A vanguard detachment dug in around the junction of Highway #1 and the road from Cotabato. That night a force of Japs supported by mortars and machineguns charged the perimeter. The assault was repulsed. Seven dead Japs were found at sunrise.

Meanwhile, the 21st RCT had embarked on an audacious amphibious thrust at Pikit by way of the Mindanao River. If successful, this movement around the right flank of the advancing 19th would cut off all Japs between Ft. Pikit and Parang.

Aboard armed LCMs, one battalion passed through the gloomy estuary of the Mindanao River and occupied the provincial capital of Cotabato. It reported many crocodiles, but no Japs. On 19th April a vanguard company, patrolling upriver beyond Lomopog, encountered a clever enemy trap.

A Moro reported that 75 Japs were encamped in a bamboo grove about 2,000 yards distant. The company pressed upon the grove and was stopped by a mortar barrage. Simultaneously, a banzai attack struck its flank. The company fell back toward the river, leaving one squad to cover the withdrawal. Crouched in tall sword grass, the squad was surrounded by Japs. However, they held their own through the night and the dawn, and killed 14 Japs on their return trip to the company.

It was then discovered that one man was missing, Pfc William Roepke, 38 years old, a replacement in his first day of combat. Out on the left flank of the company he had held his position for three hours, picking off Japs, before he became aware that his company had withdrawn and that he was alone. The sun was merciless. Heavy rains fell during the night. Roepke held his post through twenty hours, killing every Jap who looked his way. When he finally decided to shoot his way out he raised his score of dead Japs to thirteen.

End of extract from General Woodruff's narrative.

DAVAO CAMPAIGN

The combat efficiency of the 21st Regiment was good upon leaving Mindoro for Mindanao. The recent acquisition of replacements had necessitated a brief but concentrated training period. At the completion of this training period the regiment was considered ready for combat.

On 17 April the 3rd Battalion landed near the town of Baras in southern Mindanao, secured a beach-head, the town of Malabang and its airfield.

Agressive patrolling was done along the Malabang-Lake Lanao Road, and along the Malabang-Parang Road. The 1st and 2nd Battalions landed at Parang and took over the security of the beach-head there. The Regimental Commander was wounded at Parang and Lieut.Colonel Arthur Henderson, Regimental Executive, ably commanded the 21st.

On 18 April the 2nd Battalion (-E Co) commanded by Lieut.Colonel Roy Marcy made an amphibious movement from Parang up the north branch of the Mindanao River and seized Cotabato. "F" Company under Captain Wicker then moved to the junction of the north and south branch of the river. Meanwhile "E" Company, Captain Kilgoe commanding, moving up the south branch of the river, landed at Tamontako. One platoon then continued up the river contacting "F" Company. "F" Company pushed on from the junction of the two branches of the river, assaulted and took the town of Lomopog. They patrolled up the river from Lomopog to Ulandang and thence to Paidu Pulangi. Upon being relieved by the 34th Infantry the battalion reassembled at Cotabato.

The entire regiment was assembled in the Cotabato area preparatory to moving to Fort Pikit and thence overland toward Davao. After rapid movement both day and night for some 140 miles, troops were tired from lack of rest. 1 May found the regiment nearing Bago preparing to begin an offensive which was to last for fifty-one consecutive days. Colonel Verbeck had recovered from his wounds received at Parang and was again in command.

The terrain in this area was a continuous climb going north into the hinterland. There were numerous streams and deep ravines. The entire area was practically covered by abaca groves so thick, movement through them was almost impossible. The road net generally consisted of a system of parallel roads at intervals of some 3 to 4 thousand yards, running north and south with an occasional unimproved road connecting them.

For three years the Japanese had prepared and perfected the defense of this area. Knowing that any enemy attack must necessarily follow along this road net, the Japanese built innumerable pillboxes and a very elaborate system of trenches, foxholes, and spider holes. Not only had these been camouflaged by the Japanese, but by natural growth as well. It was quite often impossible to detect these emplacements when only a few feet from them. Full advantage had been taken of the dense abaca groves. Many of their emplacements were very cleverly placed in these groves. Due to the denseness of the surrounding vegetation and intense heat, movement off the roads was very limited.

During the period of operations by the 21st Infantry, 1 May - 19 June, an area 12,000 yards wide was cleared for a distance of approximately 12 miles. Elements of the 100th Japanese Division, totaling approximately 6,500 men, faced this regiment. It is known that elements of the 100th Division Artillery and the 30th Division Artillery were also operating in this area. An unusually large number of automatic weapons were employed by the enemy. Many AA guns were captured which had been used for ground action. Heavy mortars and light machine-guns were also plentiful as were 47mm AT guns. The artillery pieces consisted mainly of 75mm guns.

This offensive action was completed with great loss to the 21st Infantry. Our casualties both killed and wounded were higher than ever sustained in one battle in all the history of the 21st Infantry. These officer casualties included the Regimental Commander wounded, two battalion commanders

21st Infantry Calander in Davao Campaign
1945

22 April		Moved Parang to Cotabato
23 April		Bivouacked north shore Cotabato River
25 April		Arrived vicinity of Kabakan
29 April		Matingao
30 April		Vicinity Tuban
1 May		Arrived at Tinocol - 18 miles from Davao - Received artillery fire
2 May		Trains ambushed between Tinocal and Toril. Midnight action to relieve column.
3 May		Vicinity of Bago. Attacked Mintal. Heavy fighting.
4 May		1st Bn heavily engaged near Mintal. 2nd Bn heavily engaged on Libby Air Drome.
5 May		3rd Bn attacks north into Libby Drome area. Battle of Mintal
13 May		Libby Drome finally captured. Mintal secure after 10 days hard fighting in both areas.
14 May		1st Battalion engaged on Talomo Heights. Remainder of Rgt fighting at Mintal.
19 May		Still continuously fighting. 2nd Bn. took Tugbok.
20 May		3rd Battalion crosses Talomo River at Mintal.
29 May		End of battle at Mintal - Tugbok area.
30 May		At Lobogan
31 May		1st Battalion captured Bayabas
1 June		Beginning of continuous advance toward the north in area west of the Davao - Mintal - Tugbok area.
2 June		Took Mulig
3 June		Took Alhambre
4 June		Took Naming and Shangkee
13 June		Took Tagakpan
14 June		Took Wangan
18 June		Took Calinan
19 June		Regiment relieved from combat after 63 days of continuous fighting and attack. Moved to rest area at Dalio.
3 July		Col. Verbeck relinquished command of 21st Infantry and became Chief of Staff 24th Division.
10 July		Regiment returned to combat in Talomo Valley area.
16 July		First Battalion made last amphibious landing of World War II, Sarangani Bay Campaign.

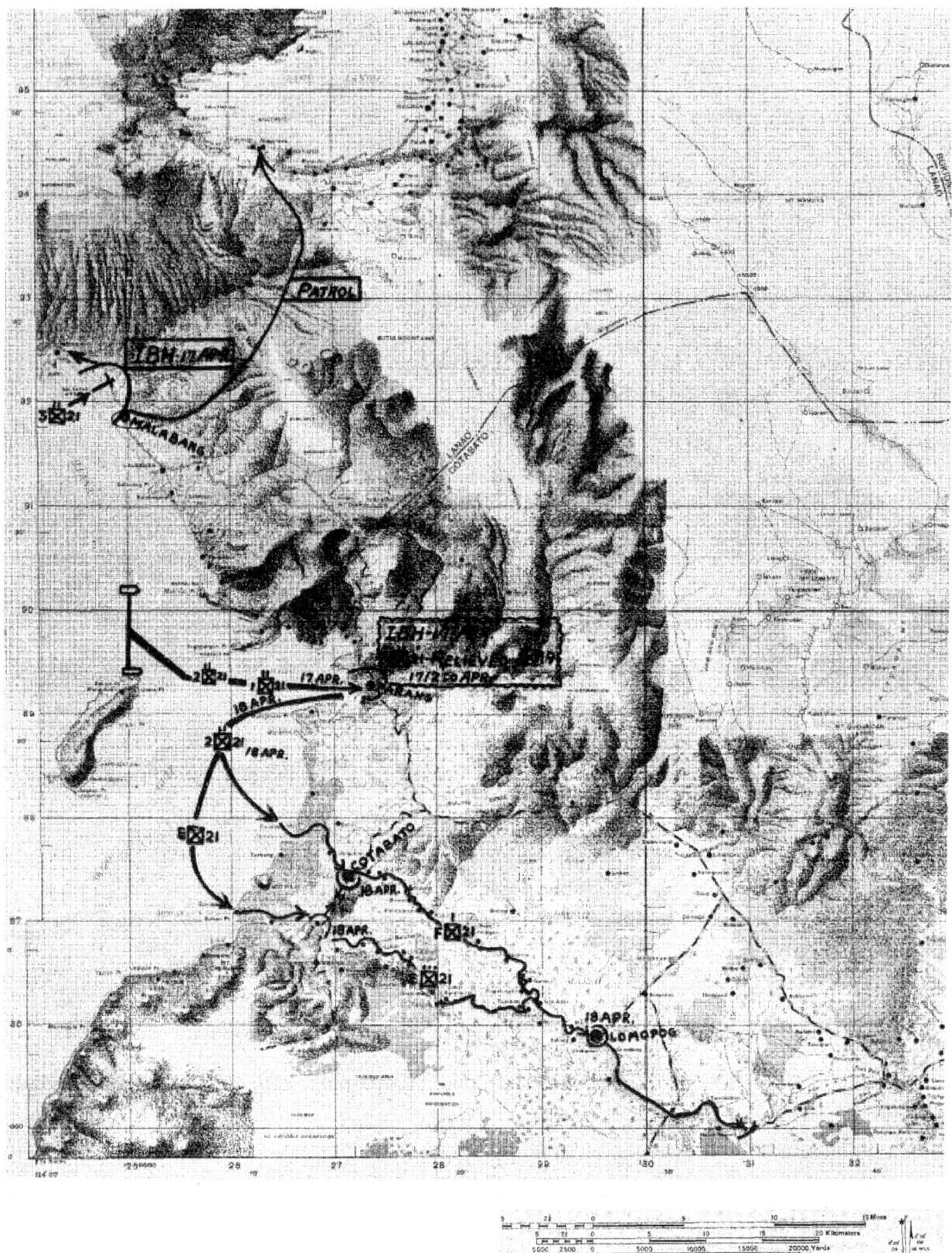

Advance during the Mindanao Campaign. Fox Company in action en route across Mindanao, April 18, 1945.

Gimlets on the march across Mindanao. April 23, 1945.

wounded, three company commanders killed, and ten company commanders wounded.

On 2 May the 1st Battalion, commanded by Major Nicholas Sloan, pushing north and west from a point 2000 yards southwest of Bago, drove within 1000 yards of Mintal. This advance was made against sporadic rifle and machine-gun fire. At the end of the day this battalion was receiving long-range artillery fire. The 2nd Battalion, moving forward from the road junction at (22.0-50.4), pushed northeast along the road to Libby Drome, then swung southeast to destroy enemy forces between it and the 2nd Battalion, 19th Infantry. At the end of the day this enemy had been forced into a small pocket near the south end of the Drome.

During the night of 2 May, the 1st Battalion repulsed two strong counterattacks. The first attack at 2100 came from the north, while the second at 0330, was directed from several points on the battalion perimeter. Known enemy dead totaled 20 KIA.

The following morning the battalion received artillery fire. Effectively placed counter-battery fire silenced the enemy positions. The battalion resumed its attack to the north against moderate small arms fire. After a sharp fire fight in the outskirts of Mintal, the battalion captured the city and pushed reconnaissance toward Tugbok.

Marcy's battalion continuing its drive to destroy enemy forces in the Libby Drome area, pushed southeast from Libby Town to within 1000 yards of the 1st Battalion, 34th Infantry, which was securing the south end of the field. The enemy well dug-in in an abaca plantation, offered strong resistance. Closely coordinated infantry, artillery and air attacks destroyed many strong points in this area.

The 3rd Battalion, commanded by Lieut.Colonel Tom Suber, relieved from Line of Communication security missions, was moving to an assembly area at a point 2500 yards southwest of Bago.

The 1st Battalion (-C Co) in the Mintal area repulsed counterattacks during the night. During the day, strong combat patrols were dispatched toward Tugbok, where they directed counter-battery artillery fire on enemy positions. Company "C", located southeast of Mintal, during the night successfully prevented enemy infiltration attempts. During the morning a strong Jap counterattack was repulsed. Thirty Japs were counted dead. The 2nd Battalion continued its assault on the enemy emplacements on the southeast end of Libby Drome. By 1200 the battalion had neutralized this resistance, established road blocks and secured the high ground in the vicinity of (27.5-54.5). The 3rd Battalion advancing northwest toward Mintal along the road on the northeast side of Libby Drome, encountered enemy emplacements and barbed wire entanglements.

The morning of 5 May Suber's Battalion contacted the enemy well entrenched in an abaca field. The 2nd Battalion was sent around the left of this battalion to flank the enemy position. As the 2nd Battalion made its attack, the 3rd Battalion pushed forward in a coordinated Infantry-Tank attack. The tanks immediately drew heavy crossfire from 57mm, 75mm and 90mm guns located in the hills on the north bank of the Talomo River. All three tanks received

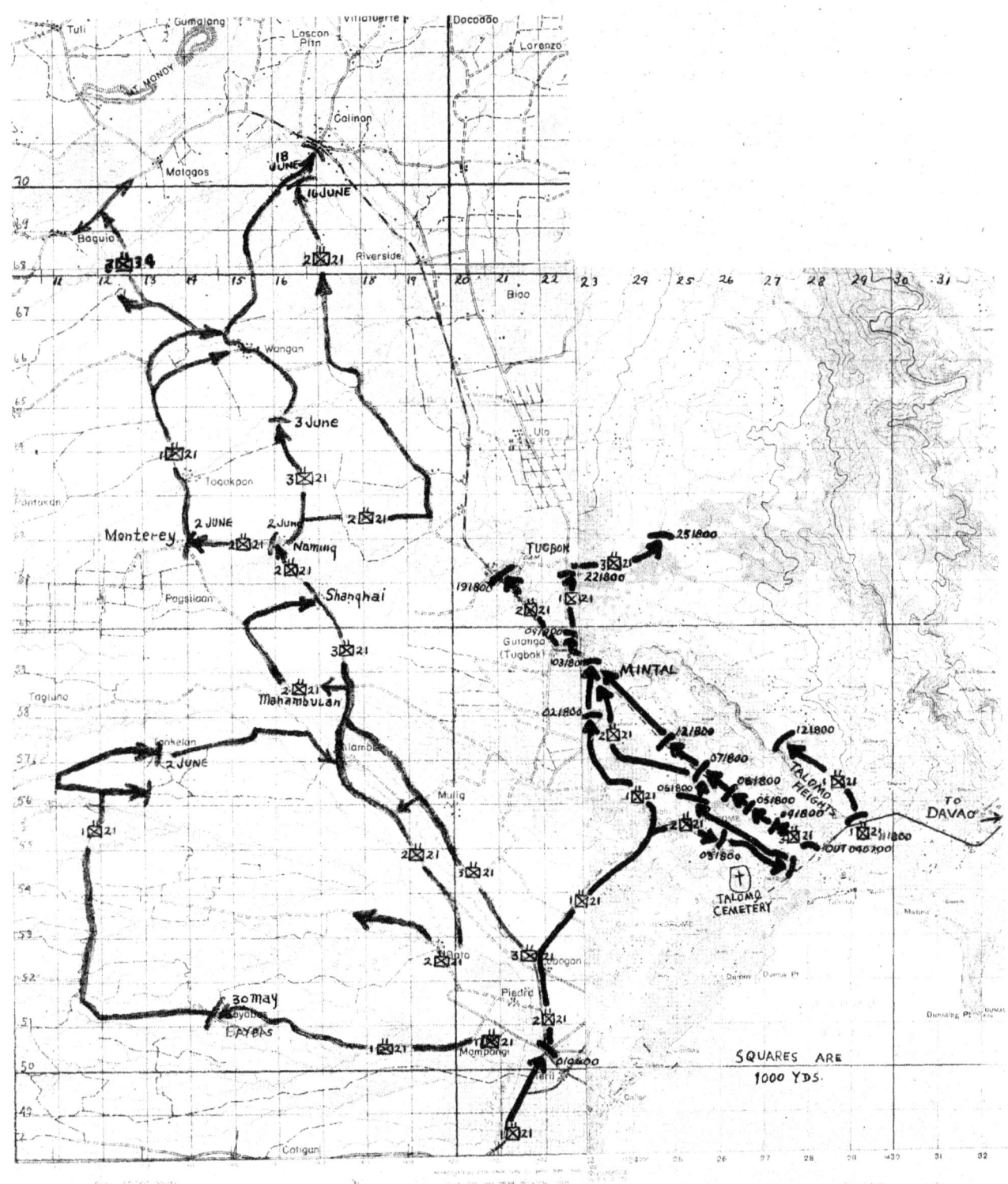

hits but were able to return under their own power. By the end of the day the 2nd Battalion had crossed the Libby Drome, and from positions on the northeast, were firing into the enemy's flank. The airfield was cleared of Japs, but the field still received enemy fire from artillery and AT gun positions located on the northeast bank of the Talomo River.

The 3rd and 2nd Battalions, following an intense artillery and air preparation attacked enemy strong-points in the abaca fields north of Libby Drome. One Jap counterattack was repulsed. Very strong resistance was met from mutually supporting pillboxes, and covered by artillery and mortar fire still coming from positions in the hills northeast of this area. Six hundred yards of ground pockmarked with enemy strong-points, were taken by the 3rd Battalion. The 2nd Battalion, protecting the left flank of the regiment, supported the attack. The 1st Battalion continued to block escape routes of the enemy to the north.

At 070645, May, the 3rd Battalion received artillery fire killing 6 men and wounding 35. Counter-battery neutralized the enemy's guns. Attacks toward Mintal continued by the 2nd and 3rd Battalions. The following day the 2nd Battalion broke through the enemy defenses and reached Mintal. One 40mm gun, one HMG and one LMG were captured and 32 Japs were killed. Meanwhile, the 3rd Battalion continued to receive enemy artillery fire from the high ground on the north bank of the Talomo River.

The 1st Battalion forced a crossing of the Talomo River north of Mintal preparatory to attacking east along Mintal-Bancal Road, to establish a roadblock in the rear of enemy forces in contact with 1st Battalion, 34th Infantry. This plan of action never materialized as the enemy resistance southeast of Mintal on the northeast bank of the Talomo River was so intense, it became necessary to abandon the 1st Battalion's bridgehead.

During the first crossing of the Talomo River, when heavy sniper fire had pinned down the forward elements, Private First Class James Diamond advanced alone, killed the first sniper and then directed the fire of a self-propelled howitzer on the pillboxes and the remaining snipers. Later he evacuated several wounded comrades across the swift, shoulder-deep Talomo River while mortar and machinegun fire raked the water and both banks. Through painfully injured, he brought the casualties to safety by driving an abandoned jeep eight times through fire so intense that all four tires were punctured.

When his battalion was ordered back, Diamond volunteered to repair the blasted Talomo River bridge. With one helper he built a foot span which enabled the battalion to withdraw across the river despite a concurrent mortar barrage. Private Diamond was killed in action on 14 May and is being recommended for the Medal of Honor.

The 1st Battalion was then moved under cover of darkness back to a position near Bancal immediately in rear of a Battalion of the 34th Infantry. The plan was to attack two Battalions abreast clearing the high ground overlooking the river and Libby Drome, thereby relieving pressure on the 3rd Battalion advancing northwest in the Drome area. This battalion repulsed a heavy grenade attack during the night.

Japanese forces in the Mintal area realizing the seriousness of their position were attacking our Mintal force, harassing them continuously in

an effort to dislodge them, before the regiment's positions were consolidated. An enemy patrol attempting to destroy a bridge in rear of the 1st Battalion along its supply route were engaged at AT Company during the night and were driven off. Eight enemy dead were counted. An estimated 100 of the enemy attacked on the morning of 11 May, 59 of whom were killed. Four LMGs and two heavy mortars were captured at this time.

The two day offensive by the 1st Battalion cleared the high ground overlooking Libby Drome, eliminating the last positions from which the enemy could bring the airstrip under fire. The 3rd Battalion, having the pressure lifted by the 1st Battalion's advance, broke through the last enemy defenses on its left flank and pushed against scattered resistance to Mintal.

Postions were consolidated and improved by aggressive patrolling in all directions. Tugbok was attacked and after two days of heavy fighting it was secured. Snipers were active north of the town and fire was being received from positions outside the town.

The 21st Infantry was given the mission of crossing the Talomo River above Mintal, driving north to the road junction at (22.7-59.8), thence northeast to cuty off the escape routes of the enemy being driven north by the 34th Infantry Regiment east of the Talomo River.

The 3rd Battalion forced a crossing of the Talomo River against exceptionally strong positions. The crossing was made under intense fire from mortars and small arms, by wading the arm pit deep river. This battalion secured the high ground overlooking this crossing. Elements of the 1st Battalion passed through the 3rd Battalion and pushed north and secured the road junction at (22.7-59.8). The 2nd Battalion remained in Tugbok, where Lt.Col. Marcy's men were engaged in fierce combat with the Japanese north and south of his position and in the town itself.

The following day the 1st Battalion pushed north toward the road junction at (22.5-61.4) encountering slight resistance until a point approximately 300 yards south of its objective was reached. Here a defense consisting of two pillboxes supported by a number of individual foxholes connected by trenches, all surrounded by a double apron fence, halted the advance. A brisk fight ensued but an attack supported by tanks overran the position and the road junction was reached. A small scale night attack at this point was repulsed. Ten Japs were killed.

The 3rd Battalion, resuming the offensive, passed through the 1st Battalion and pushed east against determined resistance. Numerous pillboxes were encountered and overrun along this road. During the night, several counterattacks were repulsed. Forty-one of the enemy were counted dead. The 1st Battalion in the vicinity of road junction (22.5-61.4) and the 2nd Battalion in Tugbok received sporadic harassing, machine-gun and mortar fire. The 3rd Battalion's forward elements reached (24.7-62.8). The order for the regiment to hold the ground it had taken was received. The gallant Lieut.Colonel Tom Suber fell seriously wounded at this point after his battalion had taken its final objective. Active patrolling in all unit sectors accounted for 25 more enemy dead. The regiment was relieved on 29 May and withdrawn to the vicinity of Lobogan.

The Regiment's job was now to drive north from Lobogan, generally along three roads, clearing the area in a zone adjoining that in which it had operated for the preceeding month.

Second Battalion, 21st Infantry following an Artillery Jeep on the march across Mindanao. April 26, 1945.

Cannon Company, M-7, S.P.M. Vehicle en-route toward Mintal, Mindanao, May 4, 1945.

Foxhole after a heavy rain Mintal, Mindanao, P.I.

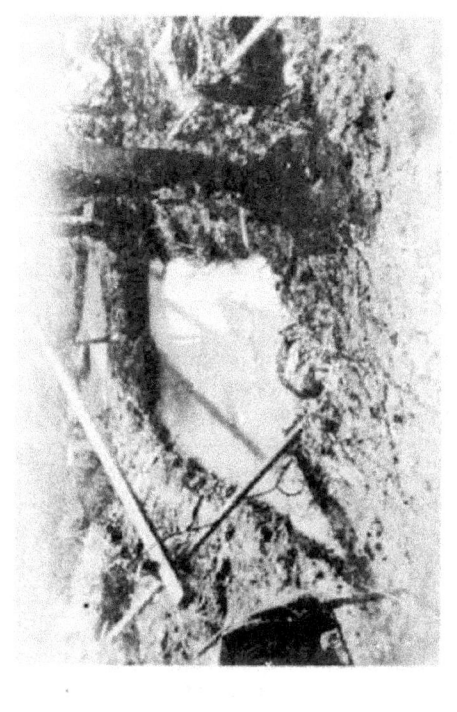

Jap 75 mm gun emplacement that overlooked Talomo airfield

Sign pointing to Mintal off the Davao, Mindanao, P.I. road.

Loading onto LCI's at Parang, Mindanao, P.I.

BRONZE STAR (OAK LEAF CLUSTER)

Captain SOTHORON K. ABLE, Infantry, United States Army. For meritorious achievement in connection with military operations against the enemy at Mindanao, Philippine Islands from 11 April to 20 June 1944. As a commander of a rifle company Captain Able contributed to a marked degree to the successful participation of an Infantry Regiment in the Mindanao operation. By his outstanding leadership, exemplary conduct and tactical ability Captain Able exerted a driving force upon his company which kept it on the initiative in spite of strong enemy resistance and heavy losses to our troops. Captain Able led and directed the advances of his company courageously and continually exposes himself to heavy enemy fire until seriously wounded on 7 May 1945. Throughout the operation he maintained coolness and composure in a manner befitting a combat company commander.

BRONZE STAR (2ND OAK LEAF CLUSTER)

Major NICHOLAS E. SLOAN, Infantry, United States Army. For heroic achievement in connection with military operations against the enemy near Mintal, Mindanao, Philippine Islands, on 10 May 1945. His battalion was order to withdraw across the Talomo River late in the evening in order to be in position for an attack the following morning. The enemy detecting the movement, put down a mortar and artillery barrage on the narrow corridor through which his troops had to move. With the field artillery liaison officer, he moved back up the ridge to a position from which they could direct our artillery fire on the enemy's position. Although enemy mortar fire was falling near his observation post, Major Sloan proceeded to adjust artillery fire upon enemy guns. The enemy fire shortly diminished to single sporadic rounds thus enabling our troops to continue an orderly withdrawal. Major Sloan's courage and resourcefulness reflect credit upon himself and the military service.

SILVER STAR (OAK LEAF CLUSTER)

Lieutenant Colonel (then Major) TOM W. SUBER, Infantry, United States Army. For gallantry in action near Mintal, Mindanao, Philippine Islands, from 4 May to 13 May 1945. Lt. Colonel Suber exhibited exceptional ability and qualities of leadership in commanding his battalion. While attacking up the road toward Mintal, the enemy had superior observation from a hill outside the battalion sector to the right flank. From this high ground, the enemy constantly subjected the troops to mortar, automatic weapons, artillery and anti-tank fire. Through the skillful tactical disposition of his men, Lt. Colonel Suber kept casualties at a minimum while continuing to drive forward. During the attack he was constantly with the front line rifle companies, under enemy observation, often subjecting himself to small arms and mortar fire in order to maintain complete control of his troops His extreme coolness under fire, even while member of his command group were wounded around him, his disregard for his own personal safety, and his determination to accomplish his mission, gave his officers and men complete confidence in his leadership. His tactical decisions were always sound and well directed. On 25

May 1945, while with one of his assault companies, Lt Colonel Suber was wounded three times by an enemy machine gun Some of his men attempted to evacuate him put he would not permit them to submit themselves to the fire, and dragged himself to safety even though seriously injured and in great pain. Lt. Colonel Suber's courage, determination and devotion to duty are a credit to himself and the military service.

SILVER STAR (Posthumous)

Second Lieutenant KEITH O. CLEMENTS, Corps of Engineers, United States Army. For gallantry in action near Mintal, Mindanao, Philippine Islands, on 15 May 1945. On this day Lieutenant Clements, a platoon commander, was making reconnaissance of a bridge to determine the possibilities of repairing the structure. The bridge was under very heavy enemy motrar fire and enemy sniper fire which made his approach to the bridge extremely difficult After cautiously working his way to the bridge site and having to take cover from enemy action, Lieutenant Clements found on arrival that crossing the river could only be accomplished by wading the swift current which was armpit deep. On the other side were several litter casualties that were in urgent need of medical care. With utter disregard for his own safety and with the help of two volunteers, Lieutenant Clements, under heavy enemy fire, improvised a foot bridge by which the patients could be brought across and thus helped in saving the lives of the men. His action in the emergency reflects the greatest credit on himself and the military service. Lieutenant Clements was later killed in action at Bunawan, Mindanao, Philippine Islands, on 22 May 1945.

BRONZE STAR

Colonel WILLIAM J. VERBECK, General Staff Corps, (then Infantry), United States Army. For heroic achievement in connection with military operations against the enemy near Bayabas, Mindanao, Philippine Islands, on 30 May 1945. On this day one company of infantry of the United States Army and one company of infantry of the Philippine Army were moving toward their objective, the town of Bayabas They were stopped approximately 1500 yards east of their objective by an enemy strong point which consisted of approximately 20 of the enemy established in a defensive position in a cave. This strong point was holding up the advance of the two entire companies with heavy machine gun fire. Upon learning the situation Colonel Verbeck, at that time a Regimental Commander, took over the command of the Filipino Company and with guerrillas as guides began a flanking move into the town through heavy abaca thickets at about 200 hours. Several times during this move they received sniper fire but reached their objective without casualties. They immediately set up a road block in the town and so successful had been their move that when six Japs, armed with a light machine gun and knee mortar, walked into the area, they were killed without loss to our forces. Due to the flanking move the strong point was cut off and the next day the American infantry company knocked out the enemy resistance which had heretofore halted the advance. This allowed them to reach their objective of Bayabas. Colonel Verbeck's heroic achievement in leading the Filipino company on this expedition reflects great credit upon himself and the military service.

FOR VALOR ON MINDANAO

Posthumous Medal of Honor Marks Four Heroic Days

WASHINGTON, March 17—The Medal of Honor has been awarded posthumously to Pfc. James H. Diamond of the Twenty-first Infantry Regiment, Twenty-fourth (Victory) Division, for four days of heroism in action, May 8, 9, 10 and 14, 1945, along the Talamo River on Mindanao in the Philippines. It will be presented to his mother, Mrs. Kate O. Diamond, of Gulfport, Miss.

Private Diamond killed a Japanese sniper and directed fire eliminating enemy pillboxes. Then, despite a wound, he evacuated wounded and repaired a bridge under heavy fire. Finally, he gave his life drawing fire to enable his patrol to reach safety.

GO 23

General Orders }
No. 23

WAR DEPARTMENT
WASHINGTON 25, D. C., 6 March 1946

	Section
MEDAL OF HONOR—Posthumous awards	I
DISTINGUISHED-SERVICE MEDAL—Award	II
DISTINGUISHED-SERVICE MEDAL (OAK-LEAF CLUSTER)—Awards	III
SILVER STAR—Award	IV
LEGION OF MERIT—Awards	V, VI
LEGION OF MERIT (OAK-LEAF CLUSTER)—Awards	VII
DISTINGUISHED-FLYING CROSS—Award	VIII
BRONZE STAR MEDAL—Awards	IX
UNITED STATES OF AMERICA TYPHUS COMMISSION MEDAL—Award	X
LEGION OF MERIT—Corrections in general orders	XI
BRONZE STAR MEDAL—Corrections in general orders and supersessions of awards	XII
BATTLE HONORS—Correction in general orders	XIII

I..MEDAL OF HONOR.—By direction of the President, under the provisions of the act of Congress approved 9 July 1918 (WD Bull. 43, 1918), a Medal of Honor for conspicuous gallantry and intrepidity at the risk of life above and beyond the call of duty was awarded posthumously by the War Department in the name of Congress to the following-named officer and enlisted man:

Private First Class *James H. Diamond* (Army serial No. 34872309), as a member of a machine-gun section, Company D, 21st Infantry Regiment, Army of the United States, displayed extreme gallantry and intrepidity on 8, 9, 10, and 14 May 1945, at Mintal, Mindanao, Philippine Islands. When a Japanese sniper rose from his fox hole to throw a grenade into their midst, this valiant soldier charged and killed the enemy with a burst from his submachine gun. Then, by delivering sustained fire from his personal arm and simultaneously directing the fire of 105-mm and .50 caliber weapons upon the enemy pillboxes immobilizing his and another machine gun section, he enabled them to put their guns into action. When two infantry companies established a bridgehead, he voluntarily assisted in evacuating the wounded under heavy fire and, securing an abandoned vehicle, transported casualties to the rear through mortar and artillery fire so intense as to render the vehicle inoperative, despite the fact he was suffering from a painful wound. The following day he again volunteered, this time for the hazardous job of repairing a bridge under heavy enemy fire. On 14 May 1945, when leading a patrol to evacuate casualties from his battalion, which was cut off, he ran through a virtual hail of Japanese fire to secure an abandoned machine gun. Though mortally wounded as he reached the gun, he succeeded in drawing sufficient fire upon himself so that the remaining members of the patrol could reach safety. Private *Diamond's* indomitable spirit, constant disregard of danger, and eagerness to assist his comrades will ever remain a symbol of selflessness and heroic sacrifice to those for whom he gave his life.

ing them with his grenades and calmly cutting down their defenders with rifle fire as they attempted to escape. When he had finished this job by sealing the four pillboxes with explosives, he had killed 20 Japanese and destroyed 3 machine guns. The advance was again held up by an intense grenade barrage which

AGO 3183B—Mar. 684256°—46

Laundry — Philipine Islands

On 30 May, Company "C" of the 1st Battalion, reinforced, moved out from Mampangi to seize and secure Bayabas. Small reconnaissance patrols operating in this area several days previous had reported considerable enemy activity. This company encountered strong resistance 2000 yards west of Mampangi. The resistance was broken, during which, two machine-gun positions were silenced. 20mm automatic fire from well dug-in positions in their flank again halted this advance. A flanking attack was made during the night, resulting in the capture of Bayabas. The following day bypassed enemy positions were eliminated, opening the road to Bayabas. Enemy entrenchments in this area were elaborate. Many pillboxes were destroyed.

"K" Company of the 3rd Battalion attacked northwest toward Alambre. Enemy contact was made at (19.5-54.7). After breaking this resistance, Alambre was captured and secured. In the meantime, Company "L" moved northwest on Mulig. Nearing the town, fire was received from road junction at (19.3-56.1). The road junction was taken and fire from four machine-guns was received from the company's right rear. Artillery and SPM fire silenced these positions.

The 1st Battalion attacked toward Tankelan (13.2-57.3) by sending "A" Company north from Bayabas and "B" Company west from Alambre. Eighteen enemy pillboxes were encountered in this drive. With Tankelan secured, "B" Company contacted and eliminated an enemy position 1000 yards northwest of Alambre.

The 2nd Battalion advancing north from Alambre pushed "G" Company west and seized Manambulan while Companies "E" and "F" pushed north and seized Shangkee. Companies "E" and "F" secured Naming and "E" Company then moved west taking Monterey. "G" Company at Manambulan pushed northwest against scattered resistance to Monterey. Patrols working east from Naming in an effort to contact the 34th Infantry at Tugbok, encountered an enemy strongpoint killing 20 Japanese.

The 1st Battalion launched an attack north from Monterey toward Tagakpan. Reaching the south bank of the river, which flows through Tagakpan, strong resistance was met. "A" Company moved up the river approximately 500 yards, made a crossing and moved north to the road, followed by "C" Company. Meanwhile, frontal pressure was maintained on the enemy by "B" Company. This crossing was made undetected. A road block was set up at the road junction (13.7-63.9). The following day, a force holding the river line in front of the 1st Battalion, was destroyed.

The regiment continued its drive toward Wangan on a three Battalion front. Sixty-six enemy dead were counted after the crossing of the river running through Tagakpan. The 1st Battalion on the left flank pushed to the road junction at (13.3-65.5), when machine-gun fire was encountered. 3rd Battalion reached road junction at (16.1-65.9). Scattered sniper fire was encountered in this move. The 2nd Battalion on the regiment's right flank pushed northwest and secured the road junction at (17.3-66.1). The Japs fought a delaying action along the road as the battalion advanced. The heavy abaca growth along both sides of the road favored these delaying actions.

Patrols sent to Wangan encountered heavy resistance and were forced to return to their units for the night. Gallant Captain Theodore Crouch, Commander of "B" Company, was killed here. His loss was keenly felt by the Regiment. The following day "A" Company secured the road junction at (14.9-66.7) and established an effective road block to ambush Japs fleeing north-

Reserve Platoon of King Company, 21st Infantry, in hastily dug positions. They were under artillery fire shortly before, from nearby high ground. Taken close to the LIBBY Airdrome near MINTAL, MINDANAO, May 7th, 1945.

I Company, 21st Infantry, going into the lines on Mindanao - June 1945.

NEWS ACCOUNTS

ACCEPTS AWARD FOR HEROIC SON - By Frank Adams, Herald State Editor. Owingsville, Ky. May 30, 1946.

The Distinguished Service Cross- the Army's second highest award for heroism in battle- was awarded posthumously here today to Capt. Theodore (Ted) Crouch who was killed in June 1945, on the island of Mindanao, in the Philippines. Arlie Crouch, father of the dead hero and superintendent of the Owingsville Cemetary, accepted the medal for his late son in the high school building here this afternoon. The medal was presented for the War Department by Col. G. T. Mackenzie, professor of Military Science and Tactics at the University of Kentucky.

Presentation of the medal and a patriotic address by state Attorney General Eldon S. Dummit of Lexington were the highlights of the communities observance of Memorial Day. The program was preceded by a parade after which several hundred citizens jammed the school auditorium for the ceremonies.

"Ted" Crouch, a graduate of Owingsville High School where he was a member of the basketball team, operated a grocery store here before he was inducted into the army in 1942. He attended Officers Candidate School and after receiving his commission was sent overseas where he served 27 months before he was killed.

Three separate demonstrations of heroic action and unusual devotion to duty were set forth in the citation accompanying the highly prized medal. The first was on May 23, 1945, when the advance of his company of the 21st Infantry Regiment of the 24th Infantry Division was halted by "heavy fire from at least eight enemy pillboxes with connecting interlocking trenches near Mintal," the citation stated.

Captain Crouch, who was the company commander, according to the citation, "stood in the road with complete disregard for his own safety, in order to direct fire against the enemy emplacements. Although intense enemy automatic fire struck down the men next to him, he located the enemy positions and then crossing the fireswept road, organized the attack and then led the assault which reduced the hostile force and killed 20 of the enemy."

"On June 2nd" the citation continued, "when sweeping enemy fire from ten pillboxes with connecting trenches halted his company near Alhambre, he called for a self propelled mount and led it forward, directing its fire against the enemy. When the mount ran out of ammunition, he called another forward and again exposing himself to the enemy fire, directed fire and observed the effects on the foe and then led the attack, which destroyed the enemy and revealed 40 enemy dead.

"On June 7, near Tagakpan, the enemy launched a surprise attack against the first battalion which threatened to disorganize its position. Capt. Crouch moved forward toward the outposts, who were withdrawing, and ignoring the raking enemy fire and rallied the men and successfully repulsed the enemy attack. He was struck and fatally wounded by a burst of fire from a hostile machine gun, but as he lay in the road he continued his skillful direction of the defense until he was evacuated.

"Through his fearless, inspiring battlefield leadership and heroic devotion to duty regardless of his own safety, Captain Crouch made a material contribution to the success of the 21st Infantry Regiment in Mindanao and upheld the finest traditions of the military service."

NEWS ACCOUNTS

NEW YORK HERALD TRIBUNE, THURSDAY, APRIL 19, 1945.
Col. William J. Verbeck, Manlius, N.Y., earned the doubtful honor of being the first American casualty of the Mindanao invasion - all because he was obeying orders to be cautious. The colonel, regimental commander in the 24th division, is known as a hard-fighting frontline soldier. He had been wounded three times before landing here. Superior officers had given him strict orders to remain at his command post, instead of rushing to the front. Four hours after the landing, a sniper - who had been lying in a nearby brush - nicked Verbeck in the back with a bullet that might have killed him had he not been leaning over at the time. As it was, he received a flesh wound and was returned to duty a few hours later. When wounded, he was sitting in his command post, per orders, several miles behind the advancing American positions.

THE EVENING STAR, WASHINGTON, D. C. Monday, June 4, 1945.
U.S. INFANTRY CHASES JAPS OUSTED FROM DAVAO INTO HILLS. Heavy fighting was under way yesterday northwest of Davao on Mindanao Island. Maj. Gen. Roscoe B. Woodruff's 24th Infantry Division pursued the ousted Davao garrison into the mountains around 10,000 foot volcanic Mount Apo. Units under Colonel William Verbeck of Brooklyn took the villages of Alhambra, Mulig and Ula. Other elements of the 24th under Col. Thomas Clifford pushed through the jungle west of Panacan.

NEW YORK TIMES. JUNE 5, 1945. GROUND TROOPS GAIN*. Elsewhere in the MacArthur Theater ground troops recorded steady gains in cleanup drives on Luzon and Mindanao Islands. Doughboys of the 24th Division straightened out their lines west of Davao City and launched a drive toward the key Mindanao town of Baguio. Working through intense heat and humidity, the troops under Maj. Gen. Roscoe B. Woodruff drove steadily through dense Abaca (hemp) groves to within 4,200 yards of Baguio, important town astride the Talomo Trail. Troops led by Col. William J. Verbeck, Manlius, N.Y., broke a strong Japanese position south of Ula after a heavy artillery and mortar barrage. More than 50 counted dead were found, indicating the enemy retreat was so hurried that they were unable to bury their dead.

west from Wangan. The 2nd and 3rd Battalions then attacked and seized Wangan. The 3rd Battalion was now commanded by Major Francis R. Dice, a veteran of every single regimental action in the Philippines. The 2nd Battalion pushed on, supported by tanks, secured ground north of the river in vicinity (17.4-67.5). Four attempts were made to force a bridgehead while subjected to heavy machine-gun and mortar fire. During an air strike, leading elements of the battalion crossed the river, while the Japs were still in a dazed condition. The 1st Battalion crossed the Talomo River assisted by fire from the 3rd Battalion. Later "I" and "K" Companies relieved the 1st Battalion of its bridgehead. To effect this relief units had to fight their way in and out of positions, accounting for 23 Japs killed.

The 3rd Battalion in its attack northwest of Wangan encountered very strong resistance at (14.8-66.8). This position was attacked twice during the day after heavy artillery concentrations had been placed on the enemy. Both attacks met heavy mortar and machine-gun fire. At the close of the day only slight gains had been made. The 2nd Battalion supported by tanks met heavy resistance at (17.2-67.5).

Agressive combat patrols eliminated enemy pockets to the regiment's front, permitting an advance toward Calinan. Stubborn enemy resistance along the way made this advance slow and hard. After meeting determined resistance at the Talomo River, a bridgehead was made. Patrols from the 2nd Battalion pushed north into Calinan, contacting elements of the 3rd Battalions, 163rd Infantry. On 18 June the 3rd Battalion pushed north and northeast toward Calinan against diminishing opposition and joined the 2nd Battalion at road junction (16.8-70.3). The following day the regiment was relieved by the 34th Infantry.

During this offensive of the 21st Infantry on Libby Airdrome and its subsequent dirve north and west it was faced by five Independent Infantry Battalions, all part of the Japanese 100th Infantry Division, plus two airfield battalions which had been converted to Infantry when the airfield were put out of commission. For the most part, these troops had occupied and trained in this immediate area for three years. Their thorough knowledge of the terrain enabled them to perfect the intricate defense system found there. They made maximum use of their weapons, their knowledge of the terrain and their commanding position throughout the campaign. Only by dogged determination, excellently coordinated air and ground attacks, and the skillful employment of all weapons, was the destruction of this force completed.

On 9 July, four Filipinos who escaped from the Japanese north of Tamogan, reported that 1,000 soldiers and more than 5,000 enemy civilians were living in the forests without food or medicines; that U. S. artillery had destroyed the last Japanese food stores in the Tamogan area; that Japanese enlisted men and civilians were willing to surrender, but that Japanese officers killed all suspected of planning to escape; and, finally, that the Japanese had taken to the practice of killing their own wounded for lack of medical supplies and surgical facilities.

On 12 July, patrols following up a report found a secret Japanese town hidden in the forests. There were many buildings, barracks, officers' quarters, a large sawmill and other equipment. Offal found on the spot indicated that the Japs had been living on jungle roots, fruit and foliage. But the beaten denizens of this community had already pulled farther into the mountains.

In the Battle for Davao, the Twenty-Fourth Infantry Division paid a heavy price. In the gorges of the Tolomo River, on the blasted precipices of Hill 550, and in the jungle-like abaca fileds between Libby Drome, Mintal and Ula, the division's teams had paid in blood for the grim satisfaction of vanquishing some of the most fanatical Japs fighting over the toughest fighting terrain on earth.

The Japs' most murderous weapons in the abaca expanses bordering Libby Drome were anti-aircraft cannon laid for level trajectory. Their shells would skim the abaca and burst in mid-air, while the riflemen weathering this holocaust could barely see beyond their sights. In addition, it was no rare occurrence that in an already decimated company twenty soldiers collapsed from heat exhaustion in the course of a single day. The 21st RCT lost two battalion commanders and twelve company commanders killed or wounded in abaca fighting.

Japanese fortifications, dug long ago, had been overgrown with natural vegetation to an extent which made them virtually invisible. The characterizations of these pillboxes by one infantry sergeant states the problem in a nutshell: "I could have walked past three pillboxes every day for a whole year and I would not have noticed them unless some Jap shot at me."

Characteristic also is the experience of a tank soldier who was blown out of his tank by a mine. He fell into an abaca thicket, and a following tank subjected him to point-blank fire, taking him for a Jap.

Japanese tunnel positions on the bank of the Tolomo River at Mintal were the most intricate every met by veteran fighting men of this division. Opening in the hillside which suggested the presence of a small cave were actually entrances to complicated tunnel systems with many openings. These tunnel mouths were often completely hidden by natural vegetation. Illustrative is the fact that one soldier, intending to flush three Japs from a cave, hurled a satchel charge which set off a tunneled ammunition dump and all but blew up the entire hill.

The Japanese who defended Davao were as fanatical a crew as ever fought a tropical war. Suicide banzai charges and night infiltration of <u>kamikaze</u> demolition units harassed all forward perimeters and lines of communication throughout the campaign. Japs invaded artillery and quartermaster perimeters, and even the division command post, with mines strapped to their bellies. Close combat night fighting with enemy suicide detachments was frequent. One soldier killed a Jap in the Tolomo River by pushing his assilant's head under water with his foot. Another pounded a Jap to death with his helmet. An officer leaning against a banana tree was impaled upon it when a Jap bayoneted him from the rear. Japs were killed with pocket knives and with bare fists. Japanese crawled to within three feet of anti-tank cannon and then jumped up to rush.

The Japs introduced two tricks, which were more effective then they would be elsewhere because the abaca fields gave them such perfect concealment for their purpose. One was for individual Japs to lie concealed in a ditch on the edge of an abaca field and slip a bangalore torpedo under the sheels of a vehicle as it passed. The other---and the hardest to stop--- was to bury or conceal 500 pound aerial bombs to which pull type igniters were attached. Then attach a rope or heavy twine to the igniter and lie concealed in a spider hole some 50 to 75 feet away---and pull the rope,

Accepts Award For Heroic Son

By J. Frank Adams
Herald State Editor

OWINGSVILLE, Ky., May 30—The Distinguished Service Cross—the Army's second highest award for heroism in battle—was awarded posthumously here today to Capt. Theodore (Ted) Crouch, who was killed in June, 1945, on the island of Mindanao, in the Philippines.

Arlie Crouch, father of the dead hero and superintendent of the Owingsville cemetery, accepted the medal for his late son in ceremonies held in the high school building here this afternoon. The medal was presented by the War Department by Col. G. T. Mackenzie, professor of military science and tactics at the University of Kentucky.

Presentation of the medal and a patriotic address by State Attorney General Eldon S. Dummit of Lexington were highlights of this community's observance of Memorial Day. The program was preceded by a parade, after which several hundred citizens jammed the school auditorium for the ceremonies.

"Ted" Crouch, a graduate of Owingsville High school where he was a member of the basketball team, operated a grocery store here before he was inducted into the Army in 1942. He attended officers' candidate school, and after receiving his commission was sent overseas where he served 27 months before he was killed.

Three separate demonstrations of heroic action and unusual devotion to duty were set forth in the citation accompanying the highly prized medal. The first was on May 23, 1945, when the advance of his company of the 21st Infantry Regiment of the 24th Infantry Division was halted by "heavy fire from at least eight enemy pillboxes with connecting interlocking trenches, near Mintal," the citation stated.

Captain Crouch, who was the company commander, according to the citation "stood in the road with complete disregard for his own safety, in order to direct fire against the enemy emplacements. Although intense enemy automatic fire struck down the men next to him, he located the enemy positions and then, crossing the fire-swept road, organized the attack and led the assault which reduced the hostile force and killed 30 of the enemy.

"On June 2," the citation continued, "when sweeping enemy fire from 10 pillboxes with connecting trenches halted his company near Alambre, he called for a self-propelled mount and led it forward, directing its fire against the enemy. When the mount ran out of ammunition, he called another forward and again, exposing himself to the enemy fire, directed fire and observed the effects on the foe and then led the attack which destroyed the enemy and revealed 25 enemy dead.

"On June 7, near Tagakpan, the enemy launched a surprise attack against the First Battalion which threatened to disorganize its position. Captain Crouch moved forward toward the outposts, who were withdrawing, and ignored the raking enemy fire and rallied the men and successfully repulsed the enemy assault. He was struck and fatally wounded by a burst of fire from a hostile machine gun, but as he lay in the road he continued his skillful direction of the defense until he was evacuated.

"Through his fearless, inspiring battlefield leadership and heroic devotion to duty regardless of his own safety, Captain Crouch made a material contribution to the successes of the 21st Infantry Regiment in Mindanao and upheld the finest traditions of the military service."

Captain Ted Crouch
Commanding Officer, Co. B,
killed in action on Mindanao.

This captured Jap Artillery Observation Post was near ULA on Mindanao. Here we see Brig. General Harry McK. Roper who commanded the X Corps Artillery, explaining his tactics to Gen's. MacArthur, Eichelberger, C.G. 8th Army and Sibert, C.G. X Corps. This is the Observation Post that directed all the fire at us in Mintal, Libby Drome and Tolomo Valley. Here it is reversed and directing fire to the North.

exploding the bomb when a remunerative target was nearby. These caused us an appreciable number of casualties, one such bomb killing 5 and seriously wounding 6 of our men. The counter measure was new type point consisting of small patrols on either side of the road some thirty or forty yards from the forward point of the advance guard on the road and 10 to 15 yards off the road. They could locate the rope, cut it---and kill the Jap in the spider hole.

An interesting situation developed near the end of the campaign when the bulk of the Japs had been driven into the hills. While in the relatively flat areas with their heavy vegetation, nearly all artillery observation on targets of opportunity was necessarily by cub plane. The Japs became accustomed to moving about in the open or on the roads when cubs were not airborne. Shortly after arrival in the higher terrain, an excel-ground OP (equipped with high powered Jap scope) was located covering an important section of a main track. Time and again, Jap working parties were caught here with VT fire with heavy casualties inflicted. The enemy apparently failed to recognize the altered OP situation.

The Japs were beaten. In seventy-four days of fighting the 24th Infantry Division had completely shattered the 100th Japanese Division and numerous auxiliary air and naval units. The enemy had joined the fight with the largest concentration of artillery which the Twenty-Fourth had encountered in four campaigns. In the course of the Davao battle 173 Japanese artillery pieces were captured or destroyed, and a great number of automatic dual purpose weapons.

Victory in Davao was the final chapter in the Philippine Liberation Campaign.

There was one more more anticlimax however. On 10 July 1945 the regiment, less the 1st Battalion, again moved up the Tamogan Trail to work over enemy remanents who were still in the field.

On the 16th of July the 1st Battalion, still commanded by Major Sloan, sailed for the final amphibious landing of the war. This was made against scattered enemy units holding Sarangani Bay. A protracted and difficult campaign of bushwacking destroyed the effectiveness of the enemy in this area to the south of the Davao Bay Region.

Just before the sailing of the 1st Battalion for Sarangani a former 1st Battalion officer, Captain William M. Langford, now Commander of M Company, was killed by enemy raiders who made a suicide rush into our rear areas. Langford was killed on the night before he was to return to the U.S. for his high point score.

Capt. Harold Edleson Killed in Action on Luzon where he commanded the Cannon Co. (Right) Lt. Col. Seymour Madison C.O. 2nd Battalion at Breakneck Ridge, Leyte, November, 1944.

Col. Thomas E. Clifford Killed in Action as Colonel of the 19th Infantry on Mindanao. Jock formerly was C.O. of 1st Bn. 21st Inf.

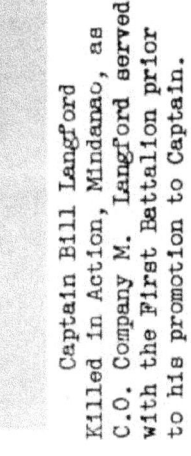

Captain Bill Langford Killed in Action, Mindanao, as C.O. Company M. Langford served with the First Battalion prior to his promotion to Captain.

HEADQUARTERS 21ST INFANTRY
Office of the Regimental Commander

APO # 24,
20 June 1945.

SUBJECT: Commendation.

TO : Officers and Enlisted Men of the 21st Infantry.

On the 19th June 1945, the 21st Infantry was withdrawn from combat and moved to a reserve area. The 18th June 1945 marked the sixty-third (63) day of continuous combat against a stubborn and well trained enemy.

During practically the entire period this regiment was attacking. Fighting in terrain which favored the enemy in defense and in hemp and cogan grass where the heat of day was radiated to an unbearable degree, you never once failed to take an assigned objective.

The 21st Infantry counted 2133 Japanese dead and captured 14 prisoners. The total for the 24th Division was 5149 enemy casualties. This regiment, therefore, accounted for 42% of the division total.

It is difficult for me to find words to express to you the admiration and respect in which I hold you. You and your dead comrades, and those of you who were wounded in action, have kindled in me an intense pride in commanding such an organization.

W. J. VERBECK,
Colonel, 21st Infantry,
Commanding.

* JAPANESE ORDER OF BATTLE, DAVAO CAMPAIGN

Elements of 100th Japanese Division	Estimated Strength
76th Infantry Brigade	
167th Independent Infantry Battalion	450
168th Independent Infantry Battalion	750
352nd Independent Infantry Battalion	750
353rd Independent Infantry Battalion	750
75th Infantry Brigade	
163rd Independent Infantry Battalion	600
Division Service Troops	1750
Division Headquarters Troops	250
Elements of Division Artillery	
Elements of 30th Division Artillery	450
12th Airfield Battalion	300
14th Airfield Battalion	300
126th Airfield Construction Unit	150

* Only those units operating in the 21st Infantry's zone of action.

Three Platoon Leader of Company "C", 21st Infantry.

    Lieut. Robert H. Malone **
    Lieut. Jack Wright *
    Lieut. Charles R. Counts

Standing near scene where first casualties of the 21st Infantry were incurred at Tanahmerah Bay, New Guinea, April 1944.

 * Killed in action - Leyte
** Wounded Leyte and Mindanao

Major Francis R. Dice
Lt. Colonel Arthur H. Henderson
Colonel William J. Verbeck
Captain Julius Berkowitz

At Toril, Mindanao, May 1945.

JOCK CLIFFORD

Lieutenant Colonel Thomas E. Clifford, Jr., commanded the 1st Battalion, 21st Infantry at Oahu, Australia, Goodenough Island and during the Hollandia Campaign. At Tanahmerah Bay, Hollandia, Dutch New Guinea Lieut. Col. Clifford distinguished himself and won the Silver Star Medal. Clifford was beloved and admired by all members of the regiment and carved out a reputation as one of the most outstanding of gimlets for all time.

During the Battle of the Ormoc Corrider when the 21st Infantry was heavily engaged at Breakneck Ridge, Lieut. Col. Clifford commanded the 1st Battalion, of the 34th Infantry Regiment of the 24th Division at Kilay Ridge where he fought one of the most remarkable engagements of the war. He was awarded the Distinguished Service Cross and promoted to Colonel and placed in command of the 19th Infantry Regiment, 24th Division.

During the Davao Campaign Colonel Clifford led his regiment in fierce combat and captured Davao City. After constant fighting Colonel Clifford was killed in action in the Davao Area on 25 June 1945, while moving forward toward his regiment's advance positions.

HEADQUARTERS X CORPS
Office of the Commanding General
APO 310

GENERAL ORDERS   7 July 1945

NUMBER   79

    The following commendation was received by the X Corps from the Commanding General, Eighth Army:

COMMENDATION

X CORPS

MAJOR GENERAL FRANKLIN C. SIBERT, COMMANDING

    It affords me sincere pleasure to extend to the officers and men of the X Corps and its attached units my deepest gratification and appreciation of their achievement in the successful operations on MINDANAO. The unswerving efforts of all commands to accomplish their missions were highlighted by the historic march of Major General Woodruff's 24th Infantry Division from Parang to Davao City, the aggressive drive of Major General Martin's 31st Infantry Division from Kabacan to Malaybalay, and the difficult advance of Brigadier General Shoe's 108th Regimental Combat Team from Macajlar Bay to Impalutao. These vigorous actions disrupted and shattered the enemy, drove him into untenable positions and rendered him incapable of any further offensive action.

    I especially wish to praise the officers and enlisted men in the smaller infantry units who overcame almost insurmountable obstacles to drive the stubbornly resisting enemy from his long established positions. Much praise is due also the members of unit staffs who planned and coordinated these arduous operations. This campaign has once again demonstrated the splendid fighting spirit of the American soldier.

                                         /s/ R. L. Eichelberger
                                         /t/ R. L. EICHELBERGER
                                              Lieutenant General, USA
                                              Commanding

BY COMMAND OF MAJOR GENERAL SIBERT:

                                              PETER SATHER, JR
                                              Colonel, GSC
OFFICIAL: Chief of Staff

    /s/ F. Nowakowski
    /t/ F. NOWAKOWSKI
        Colonel, AGD
        Adjutant General

Written upon news of Japan's surrender request. New York City, August 14, 1945.

Some are not cheering in Times Square today
Some who never again will be gay
People forget them as they sing and they dance
They're unable to be here; they haven't the chance.

Jungles of Guinea, guard well your dead
Cogon on Leyte where heros once bled
Churchyard in Lubang, hear you these cheers?
Sleep there in silence; on through the years.

Crosses on Breakneck V-day is here
Hemp fields at Davao, graveyard austere
What think you of tickertape dropped from the sky?
Do laughing and shouting, your lives glorify?

Clifford and Langford, Crouch and Bruce Hill
Do sirens and whistles give you a thrill?
Far from the shining cities gay whirl
Lie Eddleston, Davis, Diamond and Earle.

On a day in November, out there in the rain,
In mud caked fury of the Ormoc campaign
No laughing and joking lightened the scene
Sure, forget all the hardship but remember the sheen.

Revellers on Broadway what know you of grief?
Have you seen tired soldiers awaiting relief?
Have you seen all their faces when once more they move out?
Have you read in their glances that feeling of doubt?

What know you of companies of sixty or less?
Whose men never ask for help or redress
Are their lives to be forfeit if you make mistake?
Can you smile when your vitals are crushed for their sake?

Listen you reveller blowing your horn
Walk up to Mintal with me in the morn
Look over the river and see there our dead
Or would you prefer to shout "Victory" instead?

So we who are living, forget not this day
The sacrifice of heros who miss all this play
They cannot rejoin us; their duty is done
Pray for them now that victory is won.

THINGS TO REMEMBER

Condition Red Alert!
Jungle boots.
Aussie beer.
Swimming pool in Hollandia.
Jungle foot.
Christmas in Barugo.
"C" Company guarding the WACs in Tacloban.
Bridge guards along the highways.
Mud at Daro.
Mubuhay! Veectorie!
Tuba. Please bring the bottle back.
Ten in One.
General Quarters on the L.C.I.!
Carabaos.
The Carometa and Pony.
Wading ashore from the L.S.T.
Dance in the park at Calipan.
Feat at Boak.
Ambush at Gusay.
Dust in Mindoro.
Rats in San Jose.
General Cramer's inspections.
Chinese welcome in Calipan.
Jap flags for the Navy. How much?
Victory party at Lubang.
Coconuts.
Gimlet's grove.
Bongabong, Pinamalayan, Bananas and corn.
Warm canned beer.
Christmas mail in March. All smashed and wet.
The bridge over the Bugasanga River at Mindoro.
The A-20s taking off over camp.
The G.I.s
Old Soldiers Never Die.
Hello Bill - Hello Bill - This is Pappy.
The Moros and their betelnut.
Jap invasion money.
Coins in the ground at Mintal.
Red Beach.
The woodpeckers.
The hemp and the heat.
Paypayas and limes.
Rest and rehabilitation (3 days).
General Woodruff and his M-1.
Hello Nick, Hello Nick - give me a long count.
VF.
The beach at Dalio.
Lavanderas at Toril.
Diamond White six. This is Diamond six.
Hey Dice!
The Old Monk from Priory Hall.

NO MEMBER OF THE 21ST INFANTRY WAS CAPTURED OR WAS LISTED AS MISSING IN ACTION. ALL OUR DEAD WERE RECOVERED AND BURIED WITH OUR OWN.

       Your devotion to duty.

       Your undying courage.

       Your sacrifices; the hardships you underwent.

       The elan which marked you as proud men.

       Your spirit of comradeship; your cheerfulness.
       The lives you lost.
       The wounds you bear.

       Your honor.

This shall be passed to future soldiers of the Twenty-first Infantry.

This shall be given to new generations of your countrymen.

                                          W.J.V.

"The Lives you Lost - The Wounds you Bear Your Honor. This Shell be Passed--"

THE REGIMENTAL MEDICAL DETACHMENT

We members of the twenty-first Infantry Regiment who served with you in combat desire to pay you your deserved tribute here. We used to wonder in Hawaii and Australia why you held your heads high and walked as if some special respect was due you. Now we know. For we saw you laboring in the night and in the storm and in the tropic heat - labor to bring good to others, never to yourselves. You brought the brave back when the brave were no longer brave. You stopped the sands of life from flowing away from our own. We saw your cathcarts die without a murmur while saving others. When the brave assemble yonder and start to talk of their deeds - you medics will be there in the first ranks - but silent with heads high.

W.J.V.

21ST INFANTRY DECORATIONS

The following is a list of Decorations published in General Orders, 24th Division between June 1944 and December 1945. This list only contains Silver Star (SS), Bronze Star (BS), Purple Heart (PH) and Oak Leaf Cluster (C) indicating more than one award. The majority of Purple Hearts awarded to members of Infantry units are awarded in hospitals and hence do not appear in division orders. The Congressional Medal of Honor, the Distinguished Service Cross and the Legion of Merit are not published in division orders and therefore none are listed hereon.

NAME:	RANK:	ORGANIZATION:	DECORATIONS:
Aitken, Malcom D.	1st Lt.	Hq., 1st Bn.	BS
Ashe, Rob't. W.	S/Sgt.	RMD	BS
Byryus, Edward A.	T/5	RMD	PH
Able, Sothoron K.	Capt.	I Co.	BS & BSC
Adams, Wm. J.	Sgt.	A Co.	BS
Anderson, Francis W.	PFC	E Co.	BS
Adams, Roy B.	Pvt.	A.Co.	BS
Allen, Shelton P.	Maj.	S-4	BS & BSC
Adam, James	PFC	L Co.	Soldiers Medal
Baden, Albert H. Jr.	Capt.	MC	SS, BS
Birkhard, Leo J.	Pvt.	G Co.	SS
Brannen, Ed.	S/Sgt.	Hq.	BS
Banker, Charles H.	M/Sgt.	Sv.	BS
Blair, Oather	1st Lt.	AT	BS
Bracknell, Artie	Pvt.	C Co.	SS
Browning, Newton F.	Capt.	S-1	BS
Bezich, Peter N.	PFC	RMD	SS
Brock, Reinhardt W.	S/Sgt.	C Co.	SS
Babick, Peter O.	1st Lt.	1st Bn. Hq.	BS
Baker, Wm. E.	S/Sgt.	C Co.	BS
Bonton, Chas. I.	S/Sgt.	B Co.	BS
Bresnahen, John T.	PFC	D Co.	BS
Bakonyi, Leslie A.	1st Sgt.	F Co.	BS
Beeghly, Harold R.	2nd Lt.	E Co.	BS
Brodine, Glenn W.	PFC	K Co.	BS
Bates, Stanley G.	PFC	B Co.	BS
Bradshaw, Marvin M.	S/Sgt.	E Co.	BS
Baker, La Verne E.	S/Sgt.	K Co.	BS
Berry, Joy C.	Tech/Sgt.	G Co.	BS
Baughman, Joe H.	PFC	B Co.	BS
Bardick, LeGrande S.	Sgt.	I Co.	BS
Bush, Rob't. C.	Pvt.	A Co.	BS
Burton, Charles D.	T/4	D Co.	BS
Burnett, Eugene	T/5	RMD	BS
Brown, Rob't. S.	Capt.	Hq.	BS
Blaney, Kermit B.	Capt.	L Co.	BS
Berguch, Raymond C.	Pvt.	3rd Hq.	BS
Busset, Frank T.	Maj.	Hq.	BS
Boyd, Orvil	PFC	RMD	BS
Bell, Donald B.	S/Sgt.	C Co.	SS
Clifford, Thom. E.	Lt.Col.	1st Bn. Hq.	SS
Childs, John A.	Capt.	C Co.	BS
Counts, Charles R.	1st Lt.	C Co.	BS
Cox, Kenneth E.	S/Sgt.	B Co.	BS

NAME:	RANK:	ORGANIZATION:	DECORATIONS:
Campbell, Thom. R.	2nd Lt.	C Co.	SS, BS
Castle, Jamice B.	Pvt.	F Co.	BS
Coers, Burt W.	Maj.	RMD	BS
Cornfeild, Paul D.	Sgt.	C Co.	BS
Cameron, Jefferson W.	PFC	A Co.	BS
Camborn, Robert J.	S/Sgt.	L Co.	BS
Cheatwood, Wm. L.	Sgt.	K Co.	BS
Coker, Clarence E.	S/Sgt.	C Co.	BS
Castro, Dominic R.	S/Sgt.	K Co.	SS
Clemmen, Chas. E.	Pvt.	K Co.	SS
Casteneda, Francisco	PFC	F Co.	SS
Champage, Francis	Pvt.	F Co.	SS
Choly, John N.	S/Sgt.	F Co.	BS
Cooper, Clee S.	2nd Lt.	-----	BS
Casey, Jos. R.	S/Sgt.	I Co.	BS
Cantanzro, Anthony	T/Sgt.	Cn.	BS
Carmody, Rob't. J.	2nd Lt.	A Co.	BS
Childs, John A.	Capt.	C Co.	BS
Coolidge, Stanley J.	Cpl.	M Co.	BS
Distasi, Nicholas A.	S/Sgt.	C Co.	SS
Demaree, Elmer E.	PFC	C Co.	BS, SS
Diehl, George H.	PFC	A Co.	BS
Dougherty, Wm. J.	T/Sgt.	I Co.	BS
Dantzler, Le Roy	1st Lt.	AT	BS
Dice, Francis R.	Maj.	Hq.	BS
Devoursney, Martin T.	Sgt.	I Co.	BS
Erickson, Carol G.	S/Sgt.	1st Bn. Hq.	BS
Elliot, Idua W.	1st Sgt.	C Co.	BS
Eakin, Creas E.	Cpl.	M Co.	BS
Ethridge, Fredrick O.	S/Sgt.	I Co.	BS
Ender, Robert R.	Capt.	H Co.	BS
Farmer, Edward S.	1st Lt.	1st Bn. Hq.	SS
Frantz, Ralph	PFC	C Co.	BS
Francis, Lester E.	PFC	M Co.	BS
Furnian, Jack	PFC	F Co.	SS
Francher, William F.	S/Sgt.	K Co.	BS
Feebach, Charles W.	PFC	C Co.	BS
Fiew, James E.	Sgt.	C Co.	BS
Foster, Clyde A.	PFC	3rd Bn. Hq.	BS
Falcon, Keith A.	T/3	Med.	SS, BS
Gill, Thomas P.	T/Sgt.	M Co.	BS
Gasmmill, Morris L.	PFC	Med.	BS
Gregoric, George A.	PFC	Med.	SS
Garmer, Loyd P.	S/Sgt.	A Co.	BS
Gomez, Jose A.	S/Sgt.	K Co.	BS
Groteluschen, Roland	S/Sgt.	K Co.	BS
Gardner, Joaquin R.	PFC	B Co.	BS
Garza, Jose	PFC	F Co.	BS
Graham, Wilbur C.	T/Sgt.	1st Bn. Hq.	BS
Goeb, Lawerence L.	PFC	I Co.	BS
Garrison, James E.	PFC	L Co.	SS
Girardeau, John H., Jr.	Major	Hq. Co.	BS
Galac, John T.	1st Sgt.	1st Bn. Hq.	BS
Haddock, Eugene	Sgt.	C Co.	SS
Hauskins, Archie J.	Pvt.	Med.	SS
Hudson, Roger W.	2nd Lt.	Hq. Co.	BS

NAME:	RANK:	ORGANIZATION:	DECORATIONS:
Hughes, William C.	1st Lt.	A Co.	BS
Hiber, Clarence C.	Sgt.	I Co.	BS
Hull, William R.	PFC	Med.	BS
Howery, Arthur L.	S/Sgt.	C Co.	BS
Halderson, Llewellyn D.	1st Lt.	E Co.	BS
Huggins, James	PFC	B Co.	BS
Henderson, Arthur H.	Lt.Col.	Regt.Ex. Officer	BS-1st BSC- 2nd BSC
Hasket, Woodrow W.	Pvt.	E Co.	SS
Heinig, Robert J.	1st Sgt.	D Co.	BS
Howard, Enos L.	PFC	C Co.	BS
Hartman, Robert H.	PFC	G Co.	SS
Hood, William E.	Pvt.	B Co.	BS
Hall, Claude H.	1st Lt.	2nd Bn. Hq.	SS
Hamrick, J.D.	S/Sgt.	F Co.	BS
Hartman, William H.	2nd Lt.	----	BS
Hampton, Calvin E.	Pvt.	F Co.	BS
Hembrey, Charley J.	PFC	I Co.	BS
Hodgin, John V.	S/Sgt.	1st Bn. Hq.	BS
Hughes, Carlinel	T/Sgt.	3rd Bn. Hq.	BS
Hendrickson, Luther V.	PFC	Hq. Co.	BS
Hair, Palmas J.	PFC	----	BS
Hammack, Charles V.	2nd Lt.	MD	BSC
Haas, Arthur C.	1st Lt.	H Co.	BS
Higgins, Paul M.	Sgt.	1st Bn. Hq.	BS
Irons, Philip S. III	1st Lt.	1st Bn. Hq.	SS-BS-BSC
Johnson, William Jr.	S/Sgt.	E Co.	Soldiers Medal
Jullie, Lawrence A.	PFC	Hq. Co.	BS
Jankowski, Chester G.	PFC	B Co.	BS
Jasuikiewiez, Anthony J.	S/Sgt.	K Co.	SS
Jester, George L.	PFC	A Co.	BS
Jameson, Charles R.	Capt.	F Co.	SS-BS
Johnson, Dale E.	1st Lt.	----	SS
Jackowski, John	PFC	C Co.	BS
Jones, Erner	Capt.	Med.	BS
Kaljian, Ara	Pvt.	D Co.	BS
Kimbrell, James P.	PFC	1st Bn. Hq.	BS
Kilgo, Robert L.	Capt.	E Co.	SS
Kranz, Clifford T.	PFC	A Co.	BS
Keating, William A.	S/Sgt.	D Co.	BS
Kufhal, Wilbert E.	PFC	Med.	BS
Kennedy, John T.	Sgt.	I Co.	SS
Kelly, Marvin H.	S/Sgt.	A Co.	BS
Kepler, Louis G.	S/Sgt.	G Co.	SS
Kaden, Earl E.	2nd Lt.	B Co.	SS-BS
Kuehster, John E.	PFC	I Co.	BS
Kelley, Jack H.	Major	2nd Bn. Hq.	BS
Long, William N.	S/Sgt.	F Co.	Soldiers Medal
Lester, Norman R.	S/Sgt.	Hq. Co.	BS
Lyman, Charles B.	Col.	Hq. Co.	SS
Little, Laman W.	Major	2nd Bn. Hq.	BS
Madison, Seymour E.	Lt.Col.	2nd Bn. Hq.	BS
Langford, William M.	1st Lt.	D Co.	BS
Lacy, John R.	T/Sgt.	G Co.	BS
Lemkuhl, Merle E.	Pvt.	Med. Det.	SS
Letzring, Frank C.	PFC	F Co.	BS

NAME:	RANK:	ORGANIZATION:	DECORATIONS:
Liby, Chester D.	PFC	F Co.	BS
Lee, Robert E.	PFC	Med. Det.	BS
Lockhart, Gerald L.	Major	Hq. S-3	BS
Lumm, Marvin E.	PFC	3rd Bn. Hq.	BS
Luria, Sidney B.	Capt.	Med.	SS-BS
Luke, Carl K.	PFC	Med.	BS
Lenz, Hilmar W.	2nd Lt.	----	BS
Light, Andrew J.	T/Sgt.	L Co.	SS
Moye, Franklin W.	S/Sgt.	G Co.	SS
Mauriello, Angelo V.	T/5	Hq. Co.	BS
Mumper, David F.	S/Sgt.	B Co.	BS
Millirons, James L.	1st Sgt.	M Co.	BS
Meyer, Jacob	S/Sgt.	M Co.	BS
Marlett, Leal M.	PFC	Med.	BS
Mashek, John R.	T/Sgt.	K Co.	BS
Mosteiro, Francisco	PFC	K Co.	BS
Miller, Robert B.	PFC	K Co.	BS
Mott, John	Pvt.	D Co.	BS
Marcy, Roy W.	Lt.Col.	Hq.Co.	SS
Miller, George J.	Capt.	I Co.	BS
McGee, Monroe A.	Pvt.	C Co.	SS-BS
McLean, Ardell G.	1st Lt.	2nd Bn. Hq.	SS
McClelland, John W.	S/Sgt.	F Co.	SS
McGuire, Clarence R.	S/Sgt.	H Co.	BS
McNamara, Warren M.	Capt.	D Co.	BS
McKeon, Robert G.	1st Lt.	2nd Bn. Hq.	BS
Nixon, De Wayne A.	Pvt.	D Co.	BS
Nava, Jesse D.	PFC	C Co.	BS, BSC
Norman, Donald B.	Pvt.	C Co.	BS
Owen, Boyce	PFC	F Co.	BS
O'Brien, Eugene J.	S/Sgt.	1st Bn. Hq.	BS
Olivers, John P.	Sgt.	I Co.	SS
Polock, Henry	1st Sgt.	AT Co.	BS
Prestas, Andrew E.	T/Sgt.	M Co.	SS
Pietrowsky, Alex. T.	1st Sgt.	I Co.	BS
Pursley, Homer	S/Sgt.	K Co.	BS
Payne, Elva F.	T/4	C Co.	BS
Phipps, Wm.	Pvt.	F Co.	SS
Pepe, Antonia	S/Sgt.	M Co.	SS
Panting, Farrell	Pvt.	C Co.	BS
Poppa, Alvin L.	PFC	C Co.	BS
Pope, Harry D.	PFC	AT Co.	SS
Powell, James E., Jr.	PFC	C Co.	BS, BSC
Peha, Charles W.	PFC	M Co.	SS
Parent, James M.	Capt.	2nd Bn. Hq.	BS
Prodnit, Walter U.	S/Sgt.	Cn. Co.	BS
Riley, Jacob L., Jr.	Capt.	I Co.	SS
Ross, John M.	S/Sgt.	G Co.	SS
Ramee, Eric P.	Lt.Col.	3rd Bn. Hq.	SS, BS
Reese, Claude A.	1st Lt.	Hq.	BS
Rhods, Sanford S.	PFC	B Co.	BS
Reid, Niel P.	Capt.	M Co.	SS
Rockstadt, Walter E.	T/Sgt.	I Co.	PH
Rogers, Nolan E.	Pvt.	C Co.	BS
Rogers, Morgan I.	Capt.	----	BS

NAME:	RANK:	ORGANIZATION:	DECORATIONS:
Romack, Lester R.	PFC	L Co.	BS
Rosenblatt, Benjamin	1st Lt.	----	BS
Rhoda, Donald B.	PFC	E Co.	BS
Richard, Lewis	PFC	M Co.	BS
Ralston, Everett J.	PFC	C Co.	BS
Riffey, Richard G.	T/Sgt.	D Co.	BS
Rose, Homer K.	PFC	B Co.	BS
Ryan, David D.	PFC	1st Bn. Hq.	SS
Roepke, William F.	PFC	F Co.	SS
Rink, Eugene J.	T/Sgt.	AT	BS
Russell, Crawford C.	Cpl.	Med.	SS
Rochelle, Boyd L.	S/Sgt.	I Co.	SS
Rennaker, Evert D.	1st Lt.	L Co.	SS
Shapiro, Edward E.	Capt.	Med. Corp.	SS
Suber, Tom W.	Capt.	3rd Bn. Hq.	BS, SS
Short, Clarence E.	Major	Hq. Co.	BS
Sloan, Nicholas E.	1st Lt.-Capt.	Hq. Co.	BS-1st BSC-2nd BSC
Scott, John	Pvt.	C Co.	BS
Shannon, Ernest W.	PFC	B Co.	BS
Smith, Vinson S.	1st Lt.	Sv. Co.	BS-BSC
Schneeweis, Earl P.	Pvt.	C Co.	BS-BSC
Shipley, Vernon E.	S/Sgt.	D Co.	BS
Smith, Orville W.	T/5	B Co.	BS
Shaw, Frank G.	PFC	G Co.	BS
Simmons, Truman W.	PFC	L Co.	BS
Sinsel, Alvin	1st Sgt.	A Co.	BS
Sutterby, George C.	PFC	L Co.	BS
Satangelo, Carmin C.	T/4	K Co.	BS
Schappert, Joseph H.	S/Sgt.	I Co.	BS
Skrobuton, Raymond J.	PFC	AT Co.	SS
Smith, Hershel L.	PFC	A Co.	BS
Smoot, Lee R.	S/Sgt.	C Co.	BS
Stewart, Alvin E.	1st Lt.	----	BS
Stimson, Arthur E.	1st Lt.	3rd Bn. Hq.	BS
Stockert, Christ P.	PFC	A Co.	BS
Sayers, Fred P.	T/4	Med. Det.	SS
Scrapper, William, Jr.	T/Sgt.	D Co.	SS
Slaski, Alvin C.	PFC	I Co.	SS
Spero, Frank	PFC	I Co.	SS
Shook, Willard E.	PFC	C Co.	BS
Souza, Frank T.	Pvt.	D Co.	SS
Sundquist, Raymond M.	1st Lt.	Hq. Co.	BS
Smith, Cecil R.	Pvt.	AT Co.	BS
Smith, Norman K.	S/Sgt.	3rd Bn. Hq.	SS
Stein, Leonard I.	2nd Lt.	I Co.	BS
Stanford, Don D.	Major	3rd Bn. Hq.	BS
Suber, Tom W.	Lt.Col.	3rd Bn. Hq.	BSC
Seyde, Frank W.	Capt.	Hq. Co.	BS
Spencer, Clarence V.	T/Sgt.	M Co.	BS
Taylor, Leon W.	S/Sgt.	M Co.	BS
Tonelli, Raymond J.	PFC	B Co.	BS
Thompson, James H.	Capt.	----	BS
Thomas, James A.	Pvt.	Med. Det.	SS
Taylor, Melvin L.	Pvt.	M Co.	SS
Terrell, Millard C.	S/Sgt.	C Co.	BS

NAME:	RANK:	ORGANIZATION:	DECORATIONS:
Trissel, Arthur J.	2nd Lt.	D Co.	BS
Topia, Joaquin R.	Pvt.	B Co.	BS
Torres, Andres	Cpl.	M Co.	BS
Teets, Kenneth C.	S/Sgt.	K Co.	BS
Trammell, Alonzo K.	1st Lt.	H Co.	BS
Thompson, James H.	Major	3rd Bn. Hq.	BS
Underwood, Richard E.	PFC	1st Bn. Hq.	BS
Verbeck, William J.	Col.	Hq. Co.--Regt.Comd.	SS-SSC-BS-2 .PHC
Vinyard, James	T/Sgt.	A Co.	BS
Vienneau, Ernest L.	Capt.	K Co.	BS
Vaughn, Robert D.	1st Sgt.	M Co.	BS
Weber, Frederick R.	Lt.Col.	Hq. Co.	BSC
Woodville, John S.	Major	Serv. Co. S-4	BS
Whitney, Howard H.	2nd Lt.	K Co.	BS, SS
Wolf, John H.	Pvt.	L Co.	BS
Whitney, John S.	Pvt.	B Co.	BS
Witte, Frank L.	PFC	C Co.	BS
Wright, Albert J.	1st Lt.	C Co.	SS
Wingertsman, John C.	PFC	D Co.	BS
Weber, Bartholomew	S/Sgt.	A Co.	BS, BSC
Welch, Francis H.	Sgt.	L Co.	BS
Wiggins, William W.	S/Sgt.	D Co.	BS
Wilhe, Thomas W., Jr.	T/Sgt.	C Co.	BS
Woodie, Donovan K.	PFC	Med. Det.	BS
Wisor, Robert L.	1st Lt.	D Co.	BS
Wicker, Glenese	Capt.	2nd Bn. Hq.	BS
Wilson, Milton E.	Capt.	K Co.	BS
Williams, Jay B.	Capt.	3rd Bn. Hq.	BS
Youngblood, Orlan	T/Sgt.	L Co.	BS
Yarbrough, Winston	S/Sgt.	Med.	SS
Zines, Francis J.	PFC	L Co.	BS

THE FIELD OF HONOR

KILLED IN ACTION AND DIED OF WOUNDS
21st INFANTRY REGIMENT

"Before they die the brave have in their hands
a rich particular beauty for their heirs"

PROUDLY THEIR REGIMENT CLAIMS HER OWN

Capt	Langford, William M
Capt	Cathcart, John W
Capt	Crouch, Theodore
Capt	Edleson, Harold
1st Lt	Buttice, Angelo P
1st Lt	Margolis, Robert J
1st Lt	Oler, William L
1st Lt	Smith, John H
1st Lt	Holland, Woodrow W
1st Lt	Halderson, Llewelyn D
1st Lt	Wright, Albert J
1st Lt	Babich, P O
1st Lt	Hughes, W C
1st Lt	Johnson, D E
1st Lt	Pierce, J F
1st Lt	Haller, R F
1st Lt	Whitney, H H
1st Lt	Rogers, W W
1st Lt	Haas, Arthur C
1st Lt	Fourqurean, Wade B
1st Lt	Whitney, Charles R
2nd Lt	Ball, Frank H Jr
2nd Lt	Grossman, Ernest
2nd Lt	O'Brien, Donald A
2nd Lt	Prickett, Lloyd L
2nd Lt	Ward, Merlin H
2nd Lt	Rosenblatt, Benjamin
T Sgt	Light, Andrew J
T Sgt	Carey, Henry L
T Sgt	William, Clarence B
T Sgt	Rohren, E W
T Sgt	Rockstad, Walter E
T Sgt	Strittmatter, Charles J
T Sgt	Tiddemore, John W
T Sgt	Thomas, William I
T Sgt	Van Scoyk, Fred W
T Sgt	Ethridge, F O
T Sgt	Cosenza, Alfonse
T Sgt	Rohren, Edward W
S Sgt	Schmidt, R W
S Sgt	Pepe, Antonio
S Sgt	Francis, D

S Sgt	Meinlschmidt, Leonard L
S Sgt	Brown, Lawrence L
S Sgt	Demetriou, Stavros A
S Sgt	Wicker, Guy
S Sgt	Viteri, John
S Sgt	Falknor, William C
S Sgt	Francis, Donald
S Sgt	King, Ernest R
S Sgt	Ward, Wilbur
S Sgt	Robertson, Henry C
S Sgt	Shaffer, Charles M
S Sgt	Wolak, Matthew L
S Sgt	Ormerod, G
S Sgt	Kelly, F
S Sgt	Booth, F L
S Sgt	Bock, R W
S Sgt	Howery, A L
S Sgt	Keating, W A
S Sgt	Zadel, J S
S Sgt	Hibner, C C
S Sgt	Cosenza, A
S Sgt	Little, E L
S Sgt	Schmal, A J
S Sgt	Varcoe, G F
S Sgt	Stief, E W
S Sgt	Stokesberry, A C
S Sgt	Shaffer, C M
S Sgt	Long, Wm M
S Sgt	Hilary, J G
S Sgt	Phillips, J M
S Sgt	Stuke, Joseph H
S Sgt	Terrell, Millard C
S Sgt	Duffy, Robert C
S Sgt	Greene, Charles B
S Sgt	Hamrick, J O
S Sgt	Hill, Harley S
S Sgt	Fulcher, John E
S Sgt	Sloan, Daniel S
S Sgt	Kennedy, John T
S Sgt	Meyer, Jacob
S Sgt	Bohn, Alvin R
S Sgt	Schmidt, Raymond N
S Sgt	Zandel, Joseph
Sgt	Voight, Leonard
Sgt	Bolinger, Virgil E
Sgt	Breiderhoff, Joseph
Sgt	Brockish, Bernard J
Sgt	Loper, Dall L
Sgt	Cantrell, Bailus K
Sgt	Hannaford, George
Sgt	Horton, Donald
Sgt	O'Dell, Lester E
Sgt	Olmos, Marcus G
Sgt	Litaker, George M
Sgt	Olmos, Marcus
Sgt	Benson, Clifford E
Sgt	Brown, Ray P

Sgt	Rosser, Raymond
Sgt	Fike, S D
Sgt	Wiley, R F
Sgt	Fulcher, J E
Sgt	Mentzer, P W
Sgt	Corfield, P T
Sgt	Pecharich, John T
Sgt	Rastatter, David A
Sgt	Robertson, Alfred
Sgt	Smith, Glenn
Sgt	Stedham, George L
Sgt	Haught, Billy
Sgt	Holland, Omer
Sgt	Huggins, James J
Sgt	McDonald, Ray H
Sgt	Morency, Paul A
Sgt	Lopez, Fred C
Sgt	Mancini, Michael
Sgt	Miller, Neil D
Sgt	Smith, George
Sgt	Olson, Truman O
Tec 4	Fellis, Francis A
Tec 4	Mancini, Michael
Cpl	Brockman, V L
Cpl	Tierney, P J
Cpl	Fravel, Ray
Cpl	Davies, Elton H
Cpl	Fraley, Eugene L
Cpl	Okoniewski, Casimer C
Cpl	Rea, Arthur M Jr
Cpl	Showmaker, Richard M
Cpl	May, Victor J
Tec 5	Hahn, N A
Tec 5	William, J A
Tec 5	Veasey, Harry G
Tec 5	Mancini, Michael
Tec 5	Shore, R D L
Tec 5	Thornton, William
Tec 5	McGinnis, John T
Tec 5	Wroble, James L
Tec 5	Morgan, J R Jr
Pfc	Ceal, R H
Pfc	Chace, Richard M
Pfc	Cahill, Cecil H
Pfc	Burton, Francis C
Pfc	Allison, Marion
Pfc	Arbaugh, John M
Pfc	Bauer, Edward
Pfc	Blanks, John B
Pfc	Brandt, Thurman
Pfc	Caflisch, Robert J
Pfc	Cameron, Jefferson W
Pfc	Caola, John J
Pfc	Chase, James M
Pfc	Cisneros, Hector B
Pfc	Clark, Lloyd W
Pfc	Cole, Charles W

Pfc	Dahlquist, Robert G
Pfc	Diamond, James H
Pfc	Dirks, Alvin L
Pfc	Dawson, Donald
Pfc	Belhumeur, Joseph H
Pfc	Chase, J D
Pfc	Brown, Lawrence
Pfc	Carter, Forest E
Pfc	Anderson, Francis W
Pfc	Aurand, William F
Pfc	Blackstone, Charles L
Pfc	Corsi, James V
Pfc	Cekola, V A
Pfc	Cramer, R B
Pfc	Bland, H D
Pfc	Allie, C N
Pfc	Bellucco, J
Pfc	Aiello, U J
Pfc	Cook, O W
Pfc	Cottier, L R
Pfc	Byers, G
Pfc	Crow, L D
Pfc	Dunlap, John P
Pfc	Cox, William R
Pfc	Goodrich, Joseph L
Pfc	Byers, Gordon
Pfc	Adair, Godfrey C
Pfc	Artemis, Stephen
Pfc	Cramer, Robert B
Pfc	Harris, Burford H
Pfc	Fox, Charles D
Pfc	Grover, Henry A
Pfc	Felver, Carl R
Pfc	Hall, Alvin L
Pfc	Hall, Jerry B
Pfc	Helton, Raleigh B
Pfc	Feldmann, Henry G
Pfc	Grimm, Edwin F
Pfc	Howard, Lester W
Pfc	Garcia, Jesse O
Pfc	Grown, Dick
Pfc	Haugen, R E
Pfc	Heer, E C
Pfc	Hooper, R W
Pfc	Francis, L S
Pfc	Hart, F J
Pfc	Fieszel, Leroy B
Pfc	Floros, Robert F
Pfc	Foster, Homer J
Pfc	Freas, Casper J
Pfc	Gardner, Richard J
Pfc	Gardner, Wendell S
Pfc	Goeb, Lawrence L
Pfc	Gonzales, Alfred S
Pfc	Green, James V
Pfc	Grothoff, Frederick
Pfc	Hanson, Merle B

Pfc	Harris, Leonard J
Pfc	Hart, Murray C
Pfc	Havercroft, Kenneth V
Pfc	Humphrey, Donald A
Pfc	Fritzmaurice, Myron C
Pfc	Heer, Edgar C
Pfc	Lumm, M E
Pfc	Marlett, L M
Pfc	Lehmkuhl, Merle E
Pfc	Kennington, Dale O
Pfc	Moses, Donald J
Pfc	Ingram, Devon
Pfc	Kraus, James A
Pfc	Lazenby, Colquette
Pfc	Letzring, Frank C
Pfc	Morris, Robert D
Pfc	Mathis, W P
Pfc	Murphy, D M
Pfc	Long, C
Pfc	Johnson, C N
Pfc	Morgan, M K
Pfc	Jackson, C E
Pfc	McDonald, O O
Pfc	McIntyre, R W
Pfc	Laubersheimer, R A
Pfc	Lamkin, T
Pfc	Kiedrowicz, C J
Pfc	Ketterman, B
Pfc	Jackson, Donald R
Pfc	Jeskevic, Felix P
Pfc	Laughton, Clarence K
Pfc	Lewis, August H
Pfc	Luecke, Lewis J
Pfc	Marconi, Amedio P
Pfc	Merrill, James K
Pfc	Mesa, Louie
Pfc	Miller, Jacob
Pfc	Miller, Marvin
Pfc	Milstead, William
Pfc	Mikolich, Joe J
Pfc	Moore, Jack P
Pfc	Mott, John
Pfc	Jackson, Junior L
Pfc	Konarske, Robert L
Pfc	Moorehouse, Early S
Pfc	Patton, Paul
Pfc	Newman, Martin J
Pfc	Nelson, Joseph P
Pfc	Perdikakis, Gus
Pfc	Peters, Roy S
Pfc	Newell, C S
Pfc	Radcliff, Eugene
Pfc	Roseburg, D L
Pfc	Nelson, E L
Pfc	Red Tomahawk, L
Pfc	Repaskey, J
Pfc	Pinitoes, J P
Pfc	Murgas, J J

Pfc	Owens, F B
Pfc	Oliver, Thurston B
Pfc	Painter, Vermond
Pfc	Petty, Charles W
Pfc	Pinter, Joe L Jr
Pfc	Plaisance, Harris L
Pfc	Pounders, William O
Pfc	Presgraves, Frank
Pfc	Prince, Denby C
Pfc	Pritchett, Ovie J
Pfc	Ramos, Alezandro R
Pfc	Reese, Junior
Pfc	Rund, Arlo E
Pfc	Rushing, O P
Pfc	Roberts, Henry W
Pfc	Reynolds, Wayne C
Pfc	Ryers, Gorden
Pfc	Norman, Robert J Jr
Pfc	Nusdeo, Frank
Pfc	Thornhill, E L
Pfc	Thorngren, Clarence E
Pfc	Slattman, Carl H
Pfc	Vandagriff, Clifton E
Pfc	Saans, Agapito V
Pfc	Tapia, Joaquin R
Pfc	White, Robert E
Pfc	Wilder, Cecil D
Pfc	Yosten, Bernard M
Pfc	Welch, Leon A
Pfc	Woods, J D
Pfc	West, T
Pfc	Wright, G E
Pfc	Yarbro, J L
Pfc	Schroeder, E C
Pfc	Sondreal, E B
Pfc	Smith, K H
Pfc	Tedrick, R H
Pfc	Severn, R R
Pfc	Sims, W A
Pfc	Walls, M L
Pfc	Taylor, F J
Pfc	Stefanick, N
Pfc	Stoh, C R
Pfc	Shelton, L G
Pfc	Waggoner, C A
Pfc	Schfrer, M J
Pfc	Schryver, Wesley T
Pfc	Schuety, Harley V F
Pfc	Sheare, James
Pfc	Sheffhower, Joseph O
Pfc	Smagai, Stanley S Jr
Pfc	Smith, J J
Pfc	Smith, Walter R
Pfc	Smith, Willis
Pfc	Spence, Robert H
Pfc	Taylor, George H
Pfc	Talluto, Charles

Pfc	Ulrich, Frank
Pfc	Weiss, Charles F
Pfc	Torngren, Clarence E
Pfc	Smith, Glenn F
Pfc	Salazar, Don C
Pfc	Seix, Joseph H
Pfc	Riley, Gerald S
Pvt	Ciccarello, S S
Pvt	Allen, Kelly
Pvt	Earnhart, Edgar L
Pvt	Crobin, Randal R
Pvt	Baldwin, Thomas J Sr
Pvt	Bateman, Thomas
Pvt	Beckstead, Keith P
Pvt	Bowttcher, Herbert E
Pvt	Bolyard, Chester L
Pvt	Brieter, Hyman
Pvt	Cantabrana, C G
Pvt	Carl, Charles E
Pvt	Chapman, Gerald C
Pvt	Corbin, Randal R
Pvt	Cornelius, Troy L
Pvt	Kachelski, Leonard G
Pvt	Frank, Wilbur
Pvt	Asay, Winsor A
Pvt	Belyard, Chester L
Pvt	Gagliardi, Harry
Pvt	Sittler, Edwin C
Pvt	O'Neil, Timothy F
Pvt	Ortiz, Lupe G
Pvt	Parrott, Loren A
Pvt	Remiker, Arthur E
Pvt	Rising, Alfred G
Pvt	Schmidt, John
Pvt	Schuler, Darrel C
Pvt	Schulte, Melvin J
Pvt	Scott, Leroy D
Pvt	Smith, Calvin C
Pvt	Smith, Raymond
Pvt	Soloman, Darrel E
Pvt	Spak, Edward G
Pvt	Strehlmann, Leonard C
Pvt	Sullivan, James W
Pvt	Sutherland, Ray Charles
Pvt	Thompson, Robert J
Pvt	Toler, Tracy L
Pvt	Trujillo, Fred M
Pvt	Watts, Edward E
Pvt	Drake, Frank W
Pvt	Dunn, Robert E
Pvt	Duran, Lupe
Pvt	Franken, Allen C
Pvt	Fisher, Andrew L
Pvt	Flores, David
Pvt	Gildersleeve, Delvin L
Pvt	Goines, Jim B
Pvt	Gorman, Roy S

Pvt	Grassel, Albert M
Pvt	Hodges, Eugene A
Pvt	Howell, Chester L
Pvt	Huffman, Charles L
Pvt	Hyde, Harold E
Pvt	Kamai, William K Jr
Pvt	Korhonen, Andrew O
Pvt	Lawrence, Edward F
Pvt	Logan, Raymond F
Pvt	Luttrell, Peter H
Pvt	MacDonald, William G
Pvt	Martinez, Antonio C
Pvt	Messer, Walter C
Pvt	Morales, Frank G
Pvt	Nameth, James Jr
Pvt	Nelson, Orien W
Pvt	Long, Francis R
Pvt	Morgan, Melberne K
Pvt	Hartsook, Carl A
Pvt	Madrid, John V
Pvt	Richman, Richard K
Pvt	Dionne, Napoleon P
Pvt	Wooley, William J
Pvt	Woolum, Walter L
Pvt	Yococo, Paul V
Pvt	Yonis, Ralph
Pvt	Kane, J M
Pvt	Smith, John H
Pvt	O'Donnell, W
Pvt	Hartsook, C A
Pvt	Brown, L
Pvt	Hackelski, L C
Pvt	Plrmesser, L
Pvt	Ernst, J L Jr
Pvt	Haskett, W W
Pvt	Devereus, M J
Pvt	Krueger, A J
Pvt	Williams, L W
Pvt	Perri, U A
Pvt	Sherrill, M E
Pvt	Fitzmaurice, C
Pvt	Turco, M F
Pvt	Artemis, Stephan
Pvt	Collie, Delmas W
Pvt	Fitzmaurice, Myron C
Pvt	Owens, Casal T
Pvt	Cahoon, Donald E
Pvt	Coronado, Louis F
Pvt	Rubin, Glenn W
Pvt	Ahern, James F
Pvt	Causa, Luke P
Pvt	DeFoor, Herschel B
Pvt	Lang, Laverne C
Pvt	Saunders, Glenn H
Pvt	Snydar, Albert E
Pvt	Williams, Chester L
Pvt	Almonti, Dominick J

Pvt	Woodruff, Quenton C
Pvt	Matlock, Denver B
Pvt	Ballard, Jack W
Pvt	Schiffhauer, Joseph A
Pvt	Coines, Jim B
Pvt	Majchezak, Chester L
Pvt	Lowry, Herbert B
Pvt	Marano, Joseph V
Pvt	Medina, Joe
Pvt	Nusdeo, Frank
Pvt	Allie, Charles N
Pvt	Sensibaugh, Ross I
Pvt	Flanagan, William O
Pvt	Pritula, Theodore
Pvt	Mullin, Alfred E
Pvt	Rubio, Tony M
Pvt	Putnam, Ray J
Pvt	Sittler, Edwin C
Pvt	Davidson, Frank W

www.ingramcontent.com/pod-product-compliance
Lightning Source LLC
Chambersburg PA
CBHW050500110426
42742CB00018B/3319